TWENTIETH
CENTURY
WORLD
HISTORY

THE USSR
IN THE
TWENTIETH
CENTURY

PETER LANE

Principal Lecturer in History
Coloma College of Education
West Wickham, Kent

B T BATSFORD LTD *London*

CONTENTS

ACKNOWLEDGMENT

The Author and Publishers thank the following for their kind permission to reproduce copyright illustrations: Associated Newspapers Group Ltd for fig 48; Camera Press for figs 25, 37, 38, 52, 57, 62, 66 and 67; Imperial War Museum for figs 36 and 51; Keystone Press Agency for figs 32 and 64; Mansell Collection for figs 10 and 22; National Film Archive for fig 15; Novosti Press Agency for figs 4, 5, 6, 21, 26, 43-7, 54, 56, 58 and 63; Punch Publications Ltd for fig 11; Radio Times Hulton Picture Library for figs 1, 3, 7-9, 12, 14, 16, 17, 19, 20, 23, 24, 27-31, 33, 35, 39-42, 53, 55 and 60.

First published 1978
© Peter Lane 1978

ISBN 0 7134 0977 0

Printed and bound in Great Britain by Cox & Wyman Ltd, Fakenham, Norfolk for the publishers B T Batsford Ltd, 4 Fitzhardinge Street, London W1H 0AH

ON THE EVE OF THE TWENTIETH CENTURY

TSAR OF ALL THE RUSSIAS

It is difficult for us to appreciate the size of a country where the train journey from Leningrad to Vladivostok (picture 2) takes ten days. When

1 Tsar Nicholas II with his wife, who is holding the heir to the throne, the Tsarevich Alexis.

the Germans invaded Russia in 1941 (page 67) a soldier complained of 'the endless plain. One goes to sleep after a day of nothing but plain and starts off in the morning on yet another day's travel with nothing on the horizon.'

In 1900 four out of five Russians were peasants, living in small villages (picture 4). They were subjects of Tsar Nicholas II whose family, the Romanovs, had ruled since 1613. Like his predecessors, he was an autocrat; a dictator who chose his ministers, and decided Russian policy without having to bother about what the ordinary people thought or wanted. At his coronation he said: 'I will preserve the principles of the Autocracy as firmly and unswervingly as my late father.'

His wife, the Empress Alexandra (pictures 1 and 22) was the former Princess Alix of Hesse. Her mother was Princess Alice, daughter of Queen Victoria of England. Alexandra and her sister, Princess Irene of Prussia, carried the disease of haemophilia whose victims may die from the smallest accident if that causes bleeding. The females who carry this disease do not suffer from it themselves but they pass it on to the male children. Alexandra and Nicholas had four healthy daughters before they had a son, the Tsarevich Alexis. The great gift of an heir to the throne was marred by the fact that the Tsarevich suffered from haemophilia and had to be guarded day and night to prevent his having even a trivial accident. The Empress believed that only the monk Rasputin could cure her son if he became ill. This explains Rasputin's influence over her and the Tsar (p. 27).

PACIFIC OCEAN

Japan

SAKHALIN

Magadan

Vladivostok

SEA OF JAPAN

Korea

YELLOW SEA

China

Amur

Yakutsk

Lena

Lena

Bulun

Lake Baikal

Angara

Mongolia

China

Khatanga

Norilsk

Yenisey

Kuznetsk Basin

Yenisey

Peking

500 Miles

500 Kilometres

0

S i b e r i a

Ob

Ob

Omsk

Irtysh

K A Z A K H

Lake Balkhash

KIRGIZ

ARCTIC OCEAN

NOVAYA ZEMLYA

Murmansk

WHITE SEA

Archangel

Dvina

Pechora

Kama

U r a l   M o u n t a i n s

Sverdlovsk
(Ekaterinburg)

Tobol

Ural

S T A N

Tashkent

TADZHIK

Finland

Tsarskoeloe

Kronstadt

R. Neva

Leningrad
(St. Petersburg
Petrograd)

ESTONIA

LATVIA

Pskov

Kazan

Simbirsk
(Ulyanovsk)

Volga

Tsaritsyn (Stalingrad
Volgograd)

Kazakh Steppes

Amu Darya

UZBEK

Bokhara

Samarkand

TURKMEN

Oslo

BALTIC SEA

Gatchina

LITHUANIA

Brest-Litovsk

Mogilev

Kiev

Dnieper

Don

Volga

Rostov-
on-Don

Kuban

CASPIAN SEA

Baku

Iran

Britain

Poland

Warsaw

Romania

U K R A I N E

Odessa

Dniester

BLACK SEA

Sebastopol

CAUCASUS

Georgia

Tiflis

ARMENIA

Turkey

PERSIAN GULF

ARAL SEA

Ural

Arctic Circle

Arctic Circle

Moscow

▲
3 A view of Moscow in 1869, showing the Kremlin with its many domes.

◄ 2 The Soviet Union.

4 A Russian peasant woman drawing water from a well in Samara province. Notice the wooden huts, rough roof and the absence of any paving or roadway.
▼

THE ORTHODOX CHURCH

The Russian Orthodox Church supported the Tsarist regime. One of the Tsar's ministers was virtually head of the Church with the title of Chief Procurator of the Holy Synod. He saw to it that only 'reliable' people were appointed as bishops and priests, and only 'reliable' doctrines were taught in the colleges where the priests were trained. The Church dominated the lives of the people in the villages where the village priest was, perhaps, the only person who could read and write until late in the nineteenth century. Every peasant went to Church regularly, fasted when he was commanded, wore blessed medals on his own body and hung holy pictures or *ikons* in his hut (picture 5).

5 A peasant hut in the village of Kadomka, Nizhni Novgorod province, around 1900. This hut is even more primitive than those in picture 4. Russian peasants had a very hard life.

THE RUSSIAN PEASANT

On 3 March 1861, Alexander II freed the Russian peasants. Up until that time the landowners had reckoned their wealth not only in the amount of land they held but in the number of peasants they owned. Alexander II tried to help the former serfs. He set up commissions to divide up each owner's land, giving some back to the land-owner but allocating some to the peasants. To compensate the owner for the loss of land and of serfs, the peasants had to pay for their land. The land dues, as the payments were called, were to be paid for the next 49 years. To ensure that the dues were collected and paid to the government (which would then pay the owners), Alexander commanded the villagers to elect a committee in each *mir* or commune. Every peasant had to follow the decisions of the mir. It was the mir which really owned the land, not the peasant. As no peasant owned his land, he was not free to sell any. From time to time many

of the mirs re-allocated the land among their members. Unfortunately, this meant that there was no encouragement for many peasants to try to improve land they worked on since they might not have the same land in the following year.

The Russian peasant had to pay his land dues out of the money he obtained from selling crops or animals. A bad harvest, an illness in the family or some expense such as a wedding, might mean that a man would not be able to meet his dues. He could then go to the local money-lender to get what he wanted but in time would probably find himself in even greater financial trouble. Many peasants resented the fact that the allocation of land had given them, on average, only about eight acres per family, whereas when they were serfs their owners had often allowed them to farm much larger plots as their own. Many also resented the fact that their mirs had the right to re-allocate the land, and, with the increase in population, the amount given to each family tended to get smaller, as the population grew from 70 million in 1850 to 130 million by the turn of the century.

Some sons left their villages to work in the towns (p. 9). Even so, they remained — legally — members of their mir, liable for whatever taxes the mir decided to collect and for the dues payable on the family plot. Even the autocratic Alexander III (1881-94) realized that this system was not working well: the peasants were not producing enough food to feed the growing population, and they were often unable to meet the payments for land dues and money-lenders, so that they often did not have enough food for themselves. Rural poverty was widespread and the death rate among villagers was the highest in Europe. In 1882 the government set up a Land Bank, to enable peasants to borrow money at low rates of interest, and permitted a mir to make a permanent allocation of land to a family instead of re-allocating land each year. This gave the peasant a sense of permanent ownership and encouraged the more enterprising to think about improving things. The less enterprising were allowed to sell their land to the better-off peasant, or *kulak*, who then had a larger farm which enabled him to become even more successful than he had been before. But the success of the kulaks only made the harshness of the ordinary peasant's life seem all the more grim. There were frequent uprisings among peasants — against Land Captains, government tax collectors, money-lenders, owners of large estates who paid

no land dues but received compensation for the land they had lost in 1861 (p. 6) and against officials from *zemstvos* arriving to try to enforce some regulation or other.

THE ZEMSTVOS

Nicholas II had no parliament before 1905 — he was a dictator. His grandfather, Alexander II, had earned the nickname 'The Liberator' because of the many reforms he had introduced during his reign (1855-81). One of these reforms had been the setting up of a system of county and regional councils, or *zemstvos*. He divided Russia into a number of administrative districts in each of which people had to elect representatives to sit on a zemstvo which was responsible for the building of roads and bridges, and had to provide hospitals, medical services, and schools. Between 1860 and 1880 over 10 000 new schools were built by these councils.

The members of the county zemstvos elected delegates to sit on a regional zemstvo whose authority extended over a wide area, taking in a number of county zemstvos. It was the job of these regional zemstvos to ensure that the county zemstvos were carrying out their work properly. It is possible, then, to construct an incomplete pyramid to represent the democratic organizations which had been created by Alexander II. At the base of the pyramid were the peasants who elected their mirs, one for each village. Above these mirs were the county zemstvos, elected by the villagers, and above them the regional zemstvos, elected by the members of the county zemstvos. There was no top to this pyramid, since Alexander II refused to allow the election of a national council or Parliament. He was, after all, an autocrat.

Also, he saw to it that the democratically elected zemstvos were controlled. In each of the 50 provinces of European Russia there was a Tsarist-appointed Provincial Governor with the right to block any decision reached by any zemstvo in his province. There were also, lower down, District Governors and Town Commandants with similar privileges. Nicholas II's father, Alexander III took a further step against any possible stirrings of democracy in 1889 when he appointed new officials known as Land Captains. These automatically became members of local zemstvos and acted as watchdogs for the Tsar, picking out people who were politically 'unreliable', i.e. who criticised the government or the Tsar. These would then be forbidden to stand for election to any zemstvo.

INDUSTRIAL DEVELOPMENT

Until late in the nineteenth century Russia was a very under-developed country. In 1880 there were only about 950 000 men employed in industry, when Britain had about six million industrial workers. In 1855, when Britain had about 5000 miles of railway line, Russia had only one short line, running from the capital — St Petersburg — to the Tsar's winter residence of Tsarskoe Selo. There was some railway building during the reign of Alexander II (1855-81) and by 1892 Russia had about 19 500 miles of railway line.

One of Russia's problems was lack of capital for investment. Some landowners and noblemen who sold all their estates after the reforms of March 1861 (pp. 6-7) did invest some of their money, but there were not enough investing landowners. Much of the capital that was provided for the small amount of industrialization had to come from abroad. In 1872, a Welsh ironmaster, John Hughes of Dowlais, built a modern ironworks in the Donets valley in Russia; the Nobel brothers from Sweden built oil refineries in Baku and along the shores of the Caspian Sea.

Russia's industrial development did not really get under way until 1892, when the Tsar appointed a new Minister of Finance and Commerce, Sergei Witte. Witte firmly believed that Russia would always remain backward and unimportant if she did not industrialize. He also realized that Russian industrialization would have to depend for a long time on foreign capital. He organized the huge loans which Russia obtained from France from 1892 onwards, and which were first used for building the Trans-Siberian railway which took ten years to complete (1892-1902). This was only a single track line but it doubled the length of railway line in Russia.

Railway building caused an expansion in the iron and coal industries of the Donets Basin and the Ukraine. Once again it was foreigners who built the new and expanding industries. In 1909 a young peasant boy, Nikita Khrushchev, was at work. He recalled:

I worked at a factory owned by Germans, at pits owned by Frenchmen, and at a chemical plant owned by Belgians. There I discovered something about capitalists. They are all alike, whatever their nationality. All they wanted from me was the most work for the least money that would keep me alive.

There was also expansion in the textile industry, in oil production and in the number of workers employed in railway and water transport.

Few of the Tsar's ministers agreed with the industrial policies which he allowed Witte to follow. They condemned industrialization as something 'from the West', something therefore to be condemned as 'unRussian'. They feared that industrialization would lead to the growth of a new class of profit-making traders and merchants, and of an industrial working class with their roots in towns and not in the land of 'Holy Mother Russia'. The Chief Procurator of the Holy Synod, Pobedonostsev, attacked de Witte one day for talking about 'the working class';

The working class? I know of no such class in Russia, Sergei Yulevich, I do not understand what you are talking about. We have peasants. They form 90 per cent of the population. They include a relatively small number who go to work in mills and factories, but who still remain peasants. You are trying to create artificially a new class, a sort of social relationship completely alien to Russia. In this respect, Sergei Yulevich, you are a dangerous socialist.

Foreign capital had to be repaid and interest paid each year on outstanding loans. Russia had only one way of earning the foreign currency required to make these payments to foreign investors; she had to export more and more of her grain. This meant that even when there were bad harvests Russia was exporting grain, thus imposing even greater burdens on the backs of the peasant class. It is not surprising that there were those who believed that the peasant would not put up with much more and was ripe for revolution (p. 11).

6   Workers from the Putilov works, in St Petersburg (now called Leningrad), 'at home' in their barrack-like living quarters. This corner of a large room was home for the families of two workers. Notice the bedding.

8

THE INDUSTRIAL TOWNS

Many peasants left the land to seek work in the expanding towns, where they lived in overcrowded housing which lacked sanitation so that the death rate was very high. They were forced to work for long hours and low wages, and could not form trade unions or go on strike. In fact there were frequent illegal strikes. In 1897 Witte reduced the length of the working day to 11½ hours to try to appease the striking workers in St Petersburg. His failure really to understand what was happening in industrial Russia can be seen from this report from his Ministry in 1895:

> In our industry there prevail patriarchal relations between the employer and the worker. This patriarchy in many cases is expressed in the concern of the factory owner for the needs of the workers and employees in his factory . . .
> In Russia, fortunately, there is no working class in the same sense and significance as in the West, and therefore there is no labour question . . . .

Pobedonostsev was right (p. 8). It was impossible to bring Western-style industry into Russia without also importing Western-style ideas among the new classes. The mobs of urban poor listened readily to those who preached revolution (p. 10).

RUSSIAN FOREIGN POLICY

For many years Russia had adopted the policy of Pan-Slavism, the policy of 'liberating' the Slav peoples who lived under Turkish and Austrian rule. One Russian historian spoke of them in 1838 as:

> . . . the thirty million of our brothers and cousins who are scattered across the face of Europe from Constantinople to Venice . . . who are . . . bound to us in a spiritual unity by origin and language despite geographical and political separation.

In 1877-78 Russia had gone to war against Turkey in support of the Serbs who had rebelled

against their Turkish overlords. This war had ended with the signing of the Treaty of San Stefano (1878), the main feature of which was the creation of a new and very large state, Bulgaria, which was to have a section of the Aegean Sea as its southern border. The Russians must have hoped that this would be their gateway into the Mediterranean. However, the British would not accept this increase in Russian influence, while Austria feared that Russian expansion might encourage Slavs living under Austrian rule to rise up. So the representatives of the Great Powers met at the Congress of Berlin (1878) and re-drew the map of the Balkans, making Bulgaria smaller by depriving her of the coastal strip and giving Austria increased power over Bosnia and Herzegovina which Serbia had hoped to gain for herself. Russia was angry with Austria but could do nothing since Austria was supported by Germany and Britain.

Russia had been a member of the Dreikaiserbund (Three Emperors League) which had been set up by Bismarck in 1872 to make sure that France, whom Germany had defeated in a war in 1870, would have no European ally if she ever tried to make a war of revenge on Germany. But Bismarck had shown in 1878 that he favoured the other member of the league, Austria, more than Russia. It was natural that Russia should look for some other power to be her ally. The French, also looking for an ally and also opposed to the Austro-German alliance, provided Russia with most of the money required for Witte's industrialization (p. 8). The economic ties between the two countries led to closer political ties and in 1894 Russia and France signed the Dual Alliance. This said that if any country in the Triple Alliance (Germany, Austria and Italy) mobilized its forces, then the Russians and French would mobilize theirs also. This heightened the tension in Europe and made a major war more likely (p. 23).

THE FAR EAST

Having had her ambitions thwarted in the Balkans, Russia turned her attention to expansion in the east. In 1895 the Japanese waged war on the Chinese, who were forced to make many concessions to Japan. Russia signed an agreement with France and Germany to force Japan to give up some of her claims, one of

which — Port Arthur — was given to Russia by China in 1898. This was a sign of Russia's aim to acquire more power in the Far East. It also marked the beginning of that rivalry with Japan which was to lead to war in 1904 (p. 14).

REVOLUTIONARY MOVEMENTS

There were a number of revolutionary movements in nineteenth-century Russia. The Nihilists were a small group of terrorists whose aim was to destroy everything — property, officials, generals, Land Captains, buildings and industrial plants were all attacked by bombs placed by members of this group. One section of this movement, known as 'The People's Will', assassinated Alexander II on 13 March 1881. The police managed to arrest most of this group and the activities of the Nihilists were limited after this date, although one attempt was made to assassinate Alexander III. One of those executed for this attack was the elder brother, Alexander, of the 17 year-old Vladimir Ilyich Ulyanov who was at a school whose headmaster was a Mr Kerensky. The headmaster's son, Alexander Kerensky and

7 Nihilist prisoners leaving St Petersburg for Siberia, November 1879.

the young Vladimir Ilyich were to meet again in 1917 when Vladimir Ilyich, better known by his revolutionary name, Lenin, would overthrow Kerensky's government (pp. 39-40).

Populism was a movement among university students in the 1870s. They left their universities to go to the Russian villages to try and rouse the peasants to revolt against the landowners, the Tsar and the Church. In the 'mad summer' of 1874 thousands went on this pilgrimage only to find that the Russian peasant was not revolution-minded, was superstitiously submissive to Church and Tsar, and distrusted these clever young people with their weird ideas.

Although the Populist movement had fizzled out, it had a successor in the Social Revolutionary Party (SRP) which believed in the need for a peasant rising as the basis for a revolution. The SRP was founded in 1902 and its members hoped that the mir would prove to be a Russian short-cut to a Socialist society, which would enable Russia to avoid the industrial path to revolution which Marxists spoke of. One wing of the SRP also inherited some of the policies of the Nihilists and used terror as a weapon. In 1904-05 this wing claimed credit for the assassinations of the Minister of the Interior, Plehve, and of the Tsar's brother, the Grand Duke Sergei.

The Liberals hoped that Russia might become a democratically governed country, with the Tsar becoming a constitutional monarch like the British monarch. The members of the

8 The interior of the prison at Kara in Siberia. Although radicals and revolutionaries were sent here as a punishment, they used their time in study and discussion, and often became more revolutionary-minded as a result of being imprisoned.

zemstvos (pp. 7-8) gave their support to this group, hoping that constitutional reform would enable Russia to avoid the peasant revolution talked of by the SRP and the workers' revolution preached by the Marxists.

The Russian Marxists had become active in the 1890s as Russians returned from Switzerland carrying news of the work of the exile Plekhanov who had formed a Liberation of Labour group in 1883. They wanted a revolution which would lead to a Communist form of government. They believed that this revolution could only take place after Russia had undergone an industrial revolution, and would depend for its success on the unity and strength of the industrial workers. The group found ready listeners among the workers of industrial cities like St Petersburg and Moscow. In 1895 a group of Marxists, including the young Lenin, were arrested and sentenced to three years' exile in Siberia. However, in 1897,

another group of nine Marxists met in Minsk in western Russia and founded the Russian Social Democratic Labour Party (RSDLP). Lenin was not among the nine, but welcomed the news of the formation of the new party. In 1900 he went to Geneva and helped to found a newspaper, *Iskra* (the Spark), of which he boasted: 'Out of this Spark will come a Conflagration.' Time was to show how true that was. In 1903 the RSDLP split into two portions: Lenin's supporters became known as Bolsheviks ('those in the majority'), his RSDLP opponents became known as Mensheviks ('those in the minority').

9 The founders of the St Petersburg Union for the Liberation of the Working Class. Sitting, from left to right: V.V. Starkov, G.M. Krzhizhanovsky, Lenin and Y.O. Martov. Standing: A.L. Malchenko, P.K. Zaporozhets and A.A. Vaneyev.

YOUNG HISTORIAN

A

1 Give an account of life in a Russian village in 1900 to show:
   (a) how and why the mir council was elected;
   (b) the influence of the Church;
   (c) the annual allocation of land;
   (d) the payment of redemption dues.
2 Explain how the Tsar maintained his autocratic power.
3 Write an appreciation of the mir as seen by:
   (a) a disgruntled peasant;
   (b) a member of the SRP.
4 Make a list of the grievances of which Russian peasants complained in 1900.
5 Explain the reasons behind Russian industrialization. Why did most of the capital required have to come from abroad?
6 Write two paragraphs on each of the following, showing where each had their strength and how each was opposed to the other: the SRPs, the Marxists, the Liberals.

B

1 Write the letter which might have been sent by a zemstvo delegate to his village voters.

2 Write the letter which might have been sent by a friend of Nicholas II in which he talked about the assassination of Alexander II and the attempt on the life of Alexander III.
3 Write the letters in which Witte's policy is described by:
   (a) an opponent of Witte's, a friend of Pobedonostsev;
   (b) a foreign investor;
   (c) a peasant forced to pay more taxes and sell more corn;
   (d) a worker in one of the new industries.

C

Write the headlines which might have appeared above newspaper reports on:
(a) the opening of John Hughes's ironworks;
(b) the assassination of Alexander III;
(c) the coronation of Nicholas II;
(d) the formation of the SRP;
(e) the formation of the RSDLP.

D

Make an illustration with the title: 'Russia's political structure' to show the links between the peasants, the mir, and the zemstvos. Add a brief note to explain (a) why the Tsar refused to allow the election of a national parliament and (b) which group hoped for a national parliament.

FROM THE JAPANESE WAR (1904) TO WORLD WAR I (1914)

THE REASONS FOR GOING TO WAR

After 1870 the prairies of the USA were opened up and American wheat, carried on the fast new steamships, flooded the markets of Europe. The price of wheat fell by 50 per cent between 1870 and 1890. The Russian peasant had to sell more corn to get the money needed to pay land redemption dues and Witte's taxes (pp. 6-8). The various revolutionary groups tried to stir up the hungry, ill-clothed and over-taxed peasant, while the new RSDLP (p. 12) tried to create trouble among the oppressed industrial workers. In 1902 the Tsar appointed a new Minister of the Interior, Plehve, one of whose tasks was to try and root out the trouble-makers. He employed secret agents who joined the revolutionary movements and organized strikes, so that leaders of working class and peasant movements could be discovered, arrested and sentenced to imprisonment or exile.

Plehve persuaded the Tsar that 'a short, victorious war' against Japan would turn the people's attention away from their own social and economic problems, and increase popular support for the Tsar and his government. Witte, intent on Russian industrial development, opposed war, arguing that a war would mean that men and materials required for industrialization would be devoted to war purposes. It would also lead to increased taxation. But Plehve and his followers won the support of the Tsar, who dismissed Witte in 1903.

By this time Russia had expanded her trade in Manchuria and Korea and had extended her empire into Turkestan and Siberia. The Japanese wanted to have, at least, a share in the development of Korea and Manchuria. Their suggestions were ignored by the Russian government which tried to set up a Russian-controlled puppet state in Korea north of the 39th parallel. This angered the Japanese (picture 10). When Russian troops stationed in Russian-controlled Manchuria crossed the Yalu river into Japanese-dominated Korea the Japanese decided to go to war against Russia.

THE WAR, 1904-05

The war started on 4 February 1904 when the Japanese fleet made a surprise attack on the Russian fleet in Port Arthur. Two Russian battleships were sunk while still at their moorings; the rest of the great fleet was blockaded in the harbour. Another Japanese flotilla landed an invasion force to besiege the port, which eventually surrendered to the Japanese on New Year's Day, 1905.

The larger part of the Russian fleet was based in the Baltic. Although the Russian government had talked about 'a short, victorious war', no preparations had been made for such a war. The Baltic fleet was not ready to sail for the Far East until 15 October 1904. Incompetent leadership and downright ignorance hampered the fleet on its long journey. On 21-22 October, a mere week after leaving the Baltic, the fleet came across the

10 A Japanese cartoon, drawn in 1904, showing the 'Russian Octopus'. This illustrates the widespread fear of Russian power. Britain, Germany and Austria feared Russian power in Europe and the Middle East. Japan and Britain particularly feared Russian power in the Far East.

14

SWORN FRIENDS.

Russia (*aside*). "H'M—I DON'T LIKE THESE CONFIDENCES."

11 The two island nations, Britain and Japan, signed a formal alliance in 1902. Russia, represented by the figure in the background, is worried by this new development. The alliance was the result of fears of Russian aggression (picture 10) and it encouraged Japan to prepare for a war against Russia.

British herring fleet off the Dogger Bank. The Russian commander mistook the trawlers for Japanese torpedo boats and opened fire. As further confirmation of inefficiency, the Russians succeeded in sinking one of their own ships in addition to sinking one trawler, which angered Britain, Japan's ally since 1902 (picture 11). When the Russian fleet finally arrived in the Far East it was surprised by an attack as it steamed through the Straits of Tsushima on 27 May 1905. The Japanese commander reported his victory:

The above are the results of the battle which continued from the afternoon of the 27th to the afternoon of the 28th. About thirty-eight

16

of the enemy's vessels had attempted to pass the Sea of Japan, and I believe that the ships that escaped destruction or capture at our hands were limited to a few cruisers, destroyers, and special-service steamers. Our own losses in the two days' fight were only three torpedo boats. Some others of our vessels sustained more or less injuries, but not even one of them is incapacitated for future service. Our casualties throughout the whole fleet were 116 killed and 538 wounded, officers included. It cannot but be believed that the small number of our casualties was due to the protection of the spirits of the Imperial ancestors.

12 The rush of the Japanese Guards against the Russian forces at Conical Hill, in August 1904.

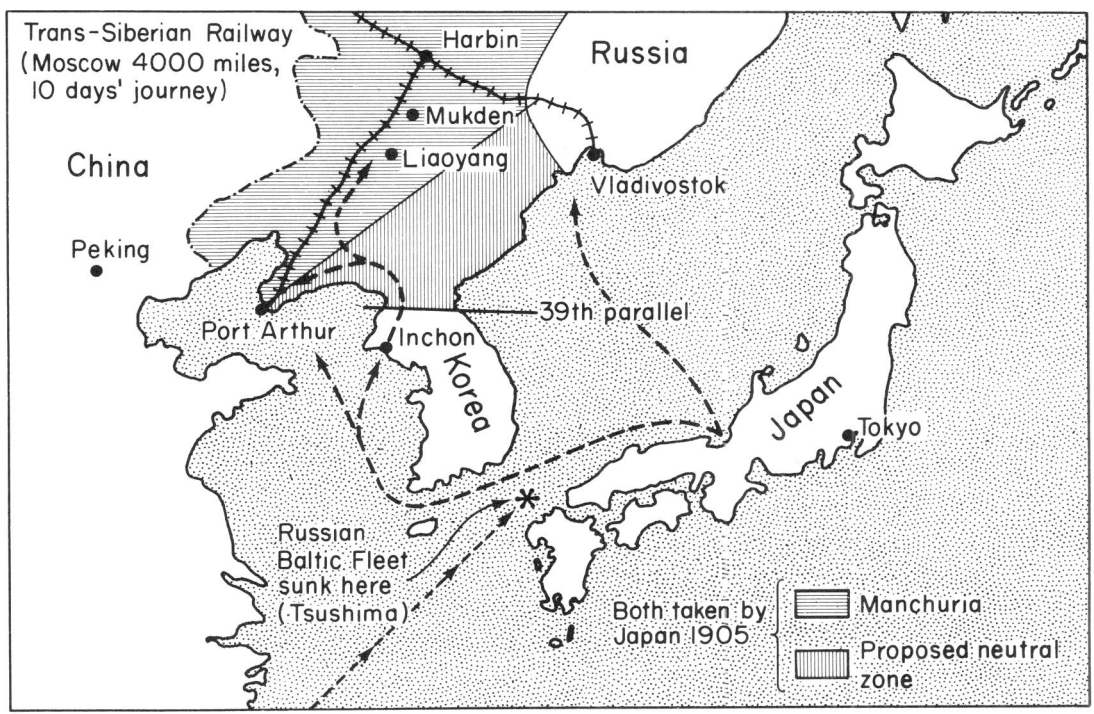

Trans-Siberian Railway
(Moscow 4000 miles,
10 days' journey)

China

Peking

Port Arthur

Inchon

Korea

Russia

Harbin

Mukden

Liaoyang

Vladivostok

39th parallel

Japan

Tokyo

Russian
Baltic Fleet
sunk here
(Tsushima)

Both taken by
Japan 1905

Manchuria

Proposed neutral
zone

13   Russia's dispute with Japan.

While the fleet was sailing to the Far East, the Russian army was engaged in bitter fighting on the Yalu river against the main Japanese army (picture 12). The Russians had to depend on the single-track line of the Trans-Siberian railway for troops, supplies and medical equipment, which took over a week to get from Moscow to Manchuria. The severe winter halted the Japanese advance and gave the Russians a chance to get a larger army together, although the best troops were kept in St Petersburg to guard against the danger of a popular uprising. In January 1905 the Russian generals decided to attack the Japanese at Mukden. The battle was a disaster. The Japanese were reinforced by the army which had succeeded in capturing Port Arthur (p. 14). The Russians were outflanked, lost over 100 000 men killed or wounded and were finally forced to surrender Mukden in March 1905.

UNREST IN RUSSIA

The war was brought to an end when both sides agreed to attend a peace conference called by President Theodore Roosevelt of the USA. The Treaty of Portsmouth, in New Hampshire, USA, was signed in September 1905 and Russia had to recognize Korea as a Japanese 'sphere of influence' and had to hand over South Sakhalin, her lease on Port Arthur.

The defeats suffered on sea and land had roused a great deal of discontent in Russia. The intellectuals (e.g. lawyers, journalists, university teachers) argued that the government which had failed so disastrously was too inefficient to be allowed to continue. Some reform was essential. The SRP, using the old-fashioned weapon of assassination, killed Plehve in 1904 and the Grand Duke Sergei in 1905. The union of the zemstvos (p. 7) proposed a number of reforms, including the right of free speech, the right to hold public meetings, the reform of the justice system to allow fair trials, and the abolition of the secret police. They also asked for the calling of a properly elected national parliament, or *Duma*. The RSDLP, at work among the industrial workers, organized a campaign of strikes and

17

demonstrations against the inefficient government which was not only losing the war, so sending working-class men to their deaths, but was also failing to cope with the problems of food distribution. The Trans-Siberian railway was unable to deal with the requirements of the military authorities as well as the demands of farmers and merchants. There was a falling-off in the amount of food available in towns so that there were bread queues, rising prices, food riots — on top of strikes in demand for higher wages and better conditions.

14   Bloody Sunday, 22 January 1905. Father Gapon and his followers come up against the royal troops outside the Winter Palace in St Petersburg.

15   A clip from the Russian film *Battleship Potemkin*, whose crew had mutinied in the harbour of Odessa on the Black Sea and hoisted the red flag of revolution. The Tsar's troops are shown attacking the rebellious sailors and their civilian sympathisers on the steps leading down to the waterfront in Odessa.

BLOODY SUNDAY, 22 JANUARY 1905

The unrest came to a head on Sunday, 22 January 1905. One of Plehve's secret agents was a Father Gapon, a priest of the Orthodox Church. He arranged with the police for a mass demonstration in the capital, St Petersburg, on 22 January 1905. On that Sunday workers from all over the capital, accompanied by their wives and children, came to the square in front of the Tsar's Winter Palace. The plan was for Father Gapon to hand a petition to the Tsar, 'the Little Father' (God being 'the Big Father'), while the people knelt in the square. The 'humble petition' — for a constitution, lower taxes, more food and trade union reform — was to be handed in on their behalf (picture 14).

At first things went as planned. The people sang hymns and carried ikons and pictures of the Tsar who had, however, left the capital. Things went wrong when the crowds refused to disperse when ordered by the police, the Cossacks and Guards. The crowd marched on, the troops opened fire and the Cossacks charged swinging their whips. Several hundred people were killed in what quickly became known as 'Bloody Sunday'.

This provoked strikes and uprisings in many

other parts of the country; peasants rioted, looted and burned; in June sailors of the Black Sea fleet took command of their battleship *Potemkin* and hoisted the Red Flag of revolution (picture 15); by October all the railwaymen were on strike, all banks were closed, school teachers came out in sympathy with the industrial workers — all this in a countrywide movement which was not organized by any of the revolutionary parties, although the members of the RSDLP had felt strong enough to set up a workers' council (or *soviet*) in St Petersburg which was dominated by the brilliant Trotsky (picture 16) until Lenin (picture 27) returned from exile in November 1905.

THE OCTOBER MANIFESTO, 1905

The failure of the policies of the war party forced the Tsar to bring back Witte in 1905. Having originally opposed the war against Japan (p. 14) he now negotiated the Treaty of Portsmouth which brought that war to an end. He then convinced the Tsar that some reforms were essential if the monarchy was to survive. Failure to reform could only lead to an increase in violence and strikes, and even greater demonstrations of workers' power. The Tsar, a virtual prisoner in the Summer Palace where he had remained since Bloody Sunday, finally agreed and issued the October Manifesto on 17 October 1905. In this he promised freedom of speech and the calling of a democratically elected parliament which would control legislation. At first this promise of reform made little difference to conditions inside Russia. Trotsky dismissed the Manifesto as 'a scrap of paper' which, he said, the Tsar would tear up when it suited him. Striking workers argued that the Manifesto gave them none of the things they had demanded — food, lower taxes, higher wages and shorter hours. Peasants, angered at falling prices, high land redemption dues and taxes, continued to riot and burn. Even soldiers from the defeated army rose in revolt at Sebastopol while others took over a large section of the Trans-Siberian railway for about three months.

One result of the October Manifesto was the formation, in 1905, of a new middle class party, the Constitutional Democrats, whose leader was the historian Paul Miliukov. From its initials (in Russian, *Ka* and *De*) this party became known as

the Kadets. This Liberal party wanted land to be taken from the landowners and re-distributed among the peasants. They believed that this would lead to a decline in peasant unrest. This land policy was too much for another group of middle class people who formed the Octobrist party under the leadership of a landlord, Rodzianko, who argued that if the October Manifesto was implemented a democratic parliament would be able to work out solutions for all Russia's problems.

PUTTING DOWN THE REVOLUTION

The Tsar had never really wanted to issue the October Manifesto. He argued later that he had issued it 'in a fever'. Neither did Witte really favour the development of a western-style democratic Russia; he was a firm believer in autocratic government. By the end of 1905 the defeated army had been brought home to reinforce the Cossacks and Guards already in St Petersburg. The peasants, after almost a year-long period of riotous behaviour, were beginning to go back to work. Witte raised a new French loan which gave the Tsar money to build industry and to re-equip his army.

When the leaders of the Kadets refused to accept his invitation to become members of a proposed coalition government, Witte listened to the extremists of the right who wanted to restore Russia to the state she had been in before the disasters of January and October. In December the leaders of the St Petersburg Soviet (picture 16) were arrested, and an uprising by Moscow workers was put down by the army. A 'Union of the Russian People' was set up by right-wing extremists and patriots who urged the Tsar to withdraw the Manifesto. Nicholas issued edicts which severely limited the powers of the Duma and the rights of the electorate. The franchise (or right to vote) was given to all Russian males, while the voters were only allowed to choose delegates who would then elect the people to represent a district in the Duma. This indirect system of election was supposed to give the landowners and peasants more chance to elect conservative, church-going members and was supposed to hinder the chances of the left-wing and radical elements. While the elections were going on Nicholas II issued his 'Fundamental Law of the Empire' in which he decreed:

20

16 The Workers' Soviet, St Petersburg, 1905. Trotsky is marked with an X. He and the rest of the Soviet were sent to Siberia once the 1905 revolution had been quelled.

The Emperor of all Russia has supreme autocratic power. It is ordained by God Himself that this authority should be submitted to not only out of fear but out of a genuine sense of duty . . . .

The apparent flirtation with democracy which had taken place in October 1905 was now at an end.

THE RUSSIAN DUMAS, 1906-14

The first Duma met in St Petersburg in May 1906, knowing that Nicholas retained control over the army, foreign policy and the system of taxation. In spite of Nicholas's efforts, the Kadets were the largest single party, with the Octobrists in second place. Nicholas then limited the powers of this Duma by declaring that he had the right to veto whatever legislation it might propose.

The Kadets asked Nicholas to amend the Fundamental Law and tried to pass legislation which would have led to the landowners losing their estates (p. 6). Nicholas simply dismissed the Duma and ordered new elections.

Witte, having now served his purpose, was once again dismissed and replaced by Stolypin as Prime Minister. Under his direction pressure was exerted to produce a more pliable Duma; many candidates were barred from standing, and thousands of voters were struck off the voting registers. Leaders of the Kadets and the left-wing parties were arrested and imprisoned. But in spite of this the composition of the Second Duma, which met in March 1907, was further to the left than the First had been.

Stolypin dissolved this Duma in June, and ordered new elections. There then followed a vigorous government campaign sometimes known as the 'Stolypin Terror'; over 200 000 people were arrested and 5000 sentenced to death, unions were dissolved, 1000 newspapers suppressed — all to affect the elections. The RSDLP were forbidden to put up candidates and in the Third Duma the Kadets were reduced to a minority. This Third Duma presented few problems for Stolypin and the Tsar, but the Kadets, the SRP and the RSDLP, prevented from playing their full part in the constitutional system, became even more involved in secret organizations, terrorism and the creation of anti-Tsarist groups among peasants and workers.

STOLYPIN AND THE LAND PROBLEM

Stolypin was 'a gifted, a complex man', who said: 'I must carry through effective reforms while I also must face revolution, resist it and stop.' He was Prime Minister until 1911 when he was assassinated by a member of the SRP in Kiev. His reforms were intended to solve the land problem which he saw as Russia's main problem.

Stolypin abolished the mir (p. 6) and transferred land ownership to the peasants individually. He set up Peasant Land Banks to make it easier for peasants to purchase their land outright and to enable the enterprising to buy up the land of their less-efficient neighbours. The gentry were encouraged to sell parts of their estates to enterprising peasants. Those peasants who sold their farms were encouraged to take part in emigration schemes aimed at peopling Siberia and Turkestan.

Stolypin hoped that these reforms would lead to the creation of a prosperous, property-owning peasantry who would have 'a stake in the country', and would therefore be less willing to listen to the Kadets, SRP and other revolutionary parties. Unfortunately his policy was not given sufficient time: he was killed in 1911 and the outbreak of war in 1914 brought the sale of land to an end. Even so, by 1914 about a quarter of the peasantry had taken advantage of his schemes. These richer peasants, or kulaks, were the ones who most strongly resisted Lenin and Stalin in the 1920s (pp. 44-62). However, the bulk of the peasants still tilled their scattered strips, using primitive methods which failed to produce enough food for the Russian towns and sufficient income for the peasants themselves. Half-starved, ill educated and frequently brutalized by drink, the majority envied or despised their hard-working kulak neighbours who often employed them as wage-earning labourers.

FOREIGN POLICY

In 1907 Russia signed an *Entente*, or understanding, with Britain who had become increasingly aware of the danger presented by the growing industrial, military and naval power of Germany under the rule of an ambitious and headstrong Kaiser. Britain had also seen how weak Russia really was, unable to defeat even the emerging and still small power, Japan. There seemed little reason for Britain to fear Russia as she had done for over 100 years.

The Entente settled the long-standing dispute over Afghanistan and the Indian border; Britain was given control of Afghanistan's foreign policy and both partners agreed to share trading rights in that country. Similarly in the Persian Gulf; Russia was given control of northern Persia while Britain was given control over the south east and the Persian Gulf where British oil-interests had been established.

Russia now had a firm ally (France), and a friendly understanding with Britain. She continued to be hostile to Austria and Germany because of Austria's ambitions in the Balkans. These ambitions seemed to be endangered by the growth of a strong nationalist movement in Serbia which supported the Pan-Slavist aims favoured by some Russians (p. 9). Serbia

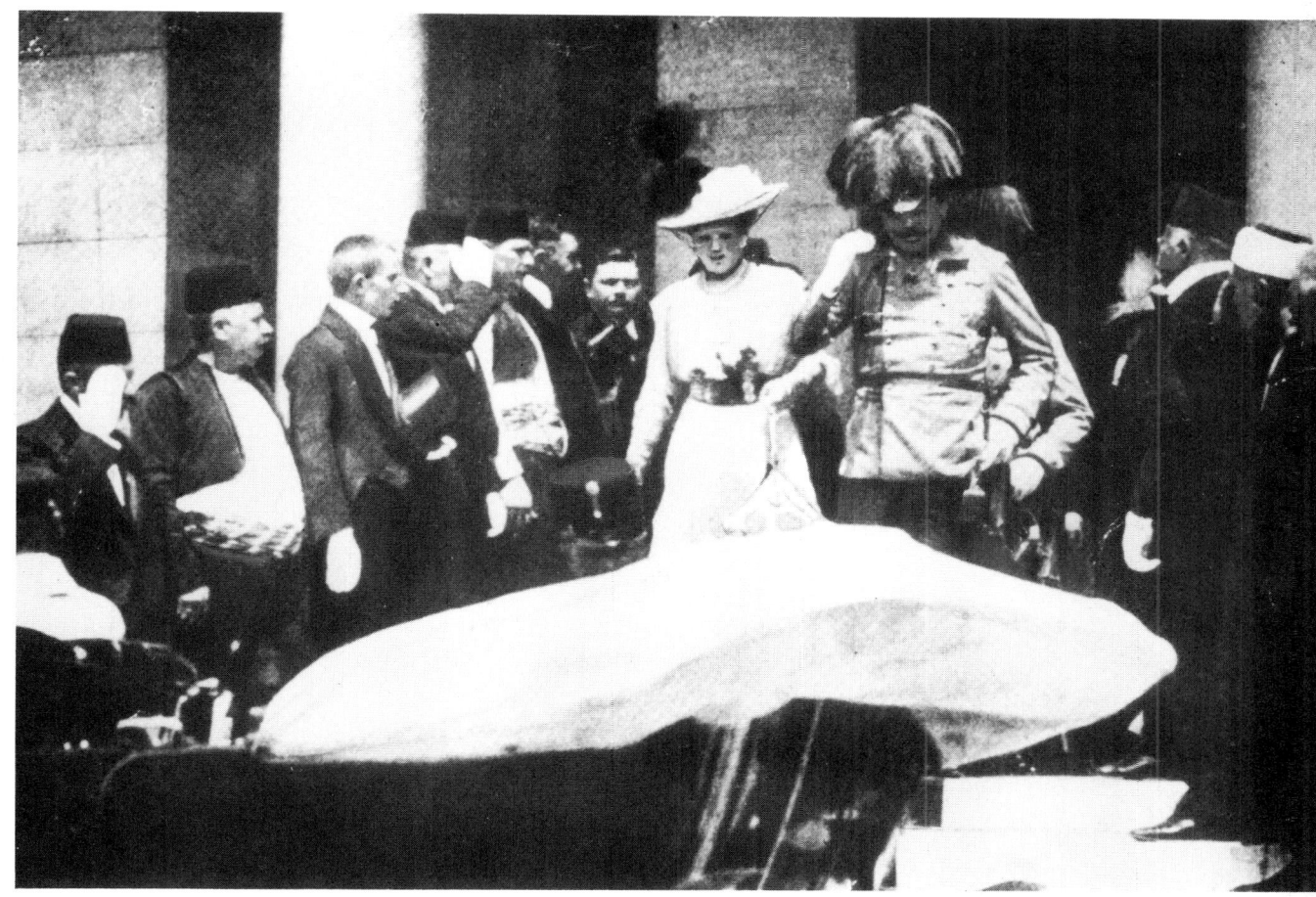

17 Archduke Franz Ferdinand and his wife shortly before the attempt on their lives.

wanted to gain control over the neighbouring Slav territories of Bosnia and Herzegovina which had been put under Austrian control in 1878 (p. 10). If this move succeeded, the Serbs hoped to link up with the Croats, Slovenes and other Slavs living in the Hungarian half of the Austro-Hungarian Empire.

The relationship between Austria and Serbia took a turn for the worse in 1908. A Young Turk revolution gave Austria the chance to annex Bosnia and Herzegovina, which angered Serbia. (In a companion volume, *Europe in the Twentieth Century*, it is explained how in 1912-13 Serbia took part in two successful Balkan wars which ended with Turkey further weakened, Serbia enlarged and even more intent on creating a new, all-embracing Slav nation.)

WORLD WAR 1, 1914

The Austrian Archduke, Franz Ferdinand, visited Bosnia in June 1914. On 28 June he was assassinated while driving through Sarajevo (picture 17). A Serbian-based nationalist group was believed to have organized this assassination and Austria used the murder as an excuse for making war on Serbia. On 23 July Austria presented Serbia with an ultimatum demanding a satisfactory answer within 48 hours. Serbia objected that to submit to Austria's demands would mean giving up her own national independence. On 28 July Austria declared war on Serbia; on 30 July the Tsar signed an order for the mobilization of the Russian army; on 1 August Germany declared war on Russia and — on 3 August — on France. World War 1 had begun.

23

A

1 Explain the grievances felt by Russian peasants (a) in 1904 before the start of the war with Japan and (b) in 1914 after Stolypin's reforms had begun to take effect. (It might be useful to take some of these headings: economic, political, taxation, social.)

2 Explain which of Russia's political parties
   (a) hoped to use the Russian peasant as the basis for a revolution;
   (b) proposed major reforms to aid the peasant;
   (c) opposed land-expropriation as a solution to the land problem;
   (d) ignored the peasant and concentrated on the industrial worker.

3 Give an account of Bloody Sunday, 1905 showing (a) why the demonstration was organized; (b) how it was conducted; (c) what the demonstrators hoped to achieve; and (d) why it ended in bloodshed.

4 Explain the widespread unrest in Russia throughout 1905, showing that (a) peasants, (b) industrial workers, and (c) intellectuals, had different reasons for their part in the anti-Tsarist campaign.

5 Explain why the Tsar issued the October Manifesto. Show how later policies tried to 'turn back the clock'.

6 Give an account of Stolypin's work, showing in particular (a) his policies towards the Tsar's powers; (b) his attempts to control the Duma; and (c) his land-reforms. How far, do you think, was his work successful?

7 Write a paragraph on each of the following: the Petrograd (St Petersburg) Soviet, 1905; Port Arthur; the Battle of Tsushima; Kadets; Sarajevo.

B

1 Write the obituary of Plehve, as it might have been written by members of (a) the SRP; (b) the RSDLP; (c) the Tsar's government.

2 Write the letters which might have been written by:
   (a) a sailor with the Baltic Fleet, 1904-5;
   (b) a Japanese explaining his fears of Russian expansion (picture 10);
   (c) one of the demonstrators who had escaped on Bloody Sunday (picture 14).

C

Write the headlines which might have appeared above newspaper reports on:
(a) the Anglo-Japanese alliance — in Russian and Japanese newspapers;
(b) the declaration of war by Japan, 1904 — in Russian and Japanese newspapers;
(c) the defeat at Mukden — in Russian and Japanese newspapers;
(d) Bloody Sunday — in newspapers controlled by the Tsar and by the RSDLP;
(e) the October Manifesto — in newspapers controlled by the Tsar, the RSDLP, the Kadets and the Octobrists;
(f) Stolypin's land reforms — in newspapers controlled by the Tsar, the RSDLP, the SRP and the Octobrists.

D

Make an illustration to go with one of the following titles:
(a) Japan defeats Russia;
(b) Russian unrest, 1905;
(c) Stolypin and the Russian peasant.

THE FALL OF THE ROMANOVS, FEBRUARY 1917

ATTITUDES TO WAR

By 1914 Stolypin's reforms were just beginning to take effect. There were already over seven million peasant proprietors, proud of their property and with a vested interest in public order. Stolypin's successors continued his policy of agrarian reform. They did not, however, recall his declaration: 'Our internal situation does not permit us to pursue an aggressive foreign policy.'

Nicholas II's ministers took Russia into the war in 1914 in spite of a memorandum by one of the ministers, Durnovo, who argued that 'Russia's probable defeat in a European War would fling the Empire into hopeless anarchy, the issue of which cannot be foreseen.' Similar warnings came from Rasputin, the Tsarina's spiritual adviser, who said: 'With the war will come the end of Russia.'

18   World War I: The Russian front against Germany and Austria.

Legend:
— August 1914
ooooo August 1915
-- December 1915
▨ Russian losses
⋰ Russian advances 1915, soon reversed

When war was declared the Tsar received the overwhelming support of his people. They rallied to the defence of their Mother Country and of their Little Father (p. 19), although he had done little for them. Even the radicals and the revolutionaries (except for the Bolsheviks) called off their campaigns 'until the war has been won'. They hoped that after the people's victory over Germany the Tsar would, in gratitude, reform the political and social system.

AT THE FRONT

By the end of 1914 there were 6 500 000 conscript soldiers in the Russian army; by 1917 over 15 million men had been enrolled. In early August they met the German army in East Prussia, won minor victories and their leaders talked of 'marching on to Berlin'. However, the German general, Ludendorff, attacked the Russians under Samsonov at Tannenberg where, at the end of August 1914, the Russians were cut off, surrounded and trapped. Millions were killed or taken prisoner (picture 19). Samsonov committed suicide and the Germans marched to the Masurian Lakes to push the last Russians out of East Prussia, although further south the Russians won a major victory at Lemberg against the incompetently led Austrians.

Throughout 1915 the German, Austrian and Russian armies fought many bitter battles along the long Eastern Front, where trenches stretched for over 800 miles. The Russian soldier was brave enough and charged when commanded, only to be mown down by enemy artillery and machine-gun fire. The Russian industrial system managed to increase production of war goods so that the men were fairly well armed; rifle production went up by 200 per cent between 1914 and the end of 1916; the output of machine guns went up

19 Russian prisoners under German guards after being captured (1915).

by 300 per cent and of artillery by 400 per cent. But there was no making good the incompetence of the Russian generals. In June 1916 General Brusilov lost a million men in an unsuccessful campaign, another million deserted and made their way home to their villages (picture 20); even those who were loyal to the Tsar began to have their doubts. Rodzianko was President of the Duma in 1914. His son, a young officer, wrote:

Things are growing worse; the men are splendid but there is a lack of grey matter in the generals' heads. We are ready to die for Russia but not for the whim of a general.

Russian incompetence can fairly be laid at the door of the Tsarina and her spiritual adviser, Rasputin, to whose every word she paid great attention. In January 1915 the Prime Minister, Kokovtsov, told the Tsar that Rasputin was an evil influence. The Tsarina persuaded her husband to dismiss Kokovtsov. His aged replacement was the 75-year-old Goremykin. The old man knew that he was not as able as the brilliant Kokovtsov; he said:

I am like an old fur coat. For many months I have been packed away in camphor. I am being taken out now for the occasion; when it has passed I shall be packed away again until I am wanted next time.

20   A loyal Russian soldier attacking one of the many deserters from the Russian army in 1917.

He was Prime Minister until 1916, when he was replaced by another of Rasputin's favourites, B.V. Sturmer, who had already proved to be an incompetent and corrupt junior minister.

The Tsar might have turned for support to the Duma which had almost formed itself into one party under the name of the Progressive Bloc led by Rodzianko, who wrote to ask the Tsar to form a ministry which would have the confidence of the Duma and the people. Once again the Tsarina interfered. In 1915 she persuaded the Tsar to dismiss the Grand Duke Nicholas from his post of Commander-in-Chief; he was too popular with the people and the Duma. She also got her husband to dissolve the Duma and dismiss all the ministers who had protested against the incompetence of Goremykin. From 1914 until 1917 there was no department in which she did not interfere. Generals were dismissed and campaign tactics were changed 'because Rasputin has had a vision'. The following extracts from some of the letters she wrote in 1915 to the Tsar give a taste of her power:

Never forget you ARE and MUST remain autocratic Emperor, we are not yet ready for a constitutional government . . . .

Deary, I heard that that horrid Rodzianko wants the Duma to be called together — oh please don't, it's not their business, they want to discuss things not concerning them and bring more discontent — they must be kept away . . . .

No, hearken unto our Friend [Rasputin]. He has your interest at heart — it is not for nothing God sent him to us — only we must pay attention to what he says . . . .

Forgive me, but I don't like the choice of the Minister of War [General Polivanov] . . . . is he not our Friend's enemy, as that brings bad luck . . . .

Now, before I forget, I must give you a message from our Friend, prompted by what he saw in the night. He begs you to order that one should advance nearer Riga, says it is necessary, otherwise the Germans will settle down so firmly for the winter that it will cost endless bloodshed and trouble to make them move . . . .

In his novel, *And Quiet Flows the Don*, Sholokhov, the Stalinist novelist, recalls what it was like on the Russian front:

The order came for the offensive to begin, and the regiments advanced. The many thousands of horses' hooves set up a deep rumbling roar that sounded as though it came from under the ground . . . . Four miles of terribly heavy going took all the strength out of the horses; some of them dropped under their riders, even the strongest stumbled, exerting all their strength to keep moving. Now the Austrian machine-guns began to work, sprinkling a hail of bullets. The murderous fire mowed down the leading ranks. A regiment of Uhlans was the first to falter and turn; a Cossack regiment broke. The machine-gun rain lashed them into panic-stricken flight. Thus this extraordinarily extensive attack was overwhelmed with complete defeat. Some of

the regiments lost half of their complement of men and horses. Four hundred Cossacks and sixteen officers were killed and wounded in Listnitsky's regiment alone.

ON THE HOME FRONT

By 1916 Russia was suffering from a desperate shortage of food. The Ukraine, the largest single corn-producing area in Russia, had been lost. Many miles of railway line had also been lost, and what remained was unable to cope with the demands of the army and munitions industries as well as with the needs of farmers (for machinery, fertilizers and animal foodstuffs) and of town merchants (who wanted to bring in corn, meat and other farm produce). In addition, the peasants were not producing as much as they might have. In part this was due to the call-up of so many active men; the women and the old men who were left behind were unable to do the work that usually was done by the soldier sons and husbands. Nor was the peasant eager to sell to the towns what little he produced. What could he buy for his corn? There were few consumer goods since industry was busy churning out war goods (p. 26).

Furthermore, the government pegged the price that the farmer got for his corn, but failed to peg other prices so that the farmer was being asked to pay ever-increasing prices for the scarce consumer goods.

By the beginning of 1917 the government had no grain reserves at all and in early March:

> . . . there were moments when the flour supply was sufficient for only a few days in Petrograd and Moscow, while there were sectors of the front with hundreds of thousands of soldiers where the bread supply was sufficient to last no more than half a day.

The townspeople, then, had little food. What was available shot up in price while the wages of industrial workers increased much more slowly:

21　Food queues in Moscow in September 1917, by which time the transport system had almost broken down so that the farmers were unable to get food into the large towns and cities. Notice the cobbled streets.

The sharpest increase in food prices occurred in the major industrial and urban centres such as Petrograd, Moscow and others. In Petrograd, prices in late 1916 increased in comparison with 1914: milk, 150 per cent; white bread, 500; butter, 830; shoes and clothing, 400 to 600 per cent.

Discontent among industrial workers and peasants was matched by growing discontent in the army (p. 27). And as Trotsky pointed out:

> The army had swollen, drawing into itself millions of workers and peasants. Every individual had his own people among the troops; a son, a husband, a brother, a relative. The army was no longer insulated, as before the war, from the people. One met with soldiers now far oftener; saw them off to the front, lived with them when they came home on leave, chatted with them on the streets and in the tramways about the front, visited them in the hospitals. The workers' districts, the barracks, the front and, to an extent the villages too, became communicating vessels. The workers would know what the soldiers were thinking and feeling. They had innumerable conversations about the war, about the people who were getting rich out of the war, about the generals, the governments, tzar and tzarina. The soldier would say about the war: To hell with it! And the worker would answer about the government: To hell with it!

POLITICAL DEVELOPMENTS, 1916-17

The Tsar refused to accept the Duma's offer of cooperation (p. 27). He allowed its members to form a Council of National Defence with Ministries of Industry, Trade and Fuel, Agriculture and Food Supplies, Transport, Navy and Finance. In their Ministry of Finance there were also representatives of the All-Russian Union of the Zemstvos which had been formed under the leadership of Prince Lvov, who was also in touch with other wartime committees formed by trade unions, local government officials and industrialists, all of whom were eager to make Russia more efficient and better able to wage war. However, all these committees and Ministries were 'shadow ministries', since they contained no member of the government. They were

22 Tsar Nicholas II (centre) with his wife (on his right), Tsarevich Alexis (on the Tsar's left) and the royal princesses. They are accompanied by a party of Russian officers. This photograph was taken in 1917 just before the revolution.

frowned on by the Tsarina and Rasputin. Of the talk of allowing the Duma and the people to have some say in the running of their country, she wrote:

> How they all need to feel an iron will and hand — you are the Lord and Master in Russia and God Almighty placed you there and they shall bow down before your wisdom and firmness.

But the Tsarina's letters did not stop the members of the Duma, the zemstvos, unions and business organizations from meeting. And when they met they talked about the government, the Tsarina — often referred to as 'the German woman', — and her friend Rasputin. After August 1915 the power of these last two increased because the Tsar foolishly took command of the Russian army and went to live at the army headquarters at Mogilev. Here he was even further out of touch with what was going on in the capital, now renamed Petrograd, and even more the victim of his wife's influence.

He may have been unaware of the increasing number of food riots which broke out during 1916 and of the brutal way in which the Cossacks put them down. He ignored the warning given by the leader of the Kadets, Miliukov, who told the Duma in November 1916 that the government was failing and that only major reform could stave off a revolution. He could not have ignored the anger against Rasputin which

30

led to his murder in December 1916 by Prince Felix Yousoupoff, who fed him with poisoned biscuit and wine, and when the cyanide failed:

> I realized that the hour had come .... I slowly raised the revolver .... I aimed at his heart and pulled the trigger. Rasputin gave a wild scream and crumpled up on the bear-skin ....

> Rasputin was dead ...

> Dimitri, Soukhotin and Doctor Lazovert ... wrapped the corpse in linen, shoved it into the car, and drove to Petrovski Island. There from the top of the bridge, they hurled it into the river.

THE 'FEBRUARY DAYS', 1917

On the British calendar the 'February Days' were 7 - 15 March! The new style of dating adopted in Britain in 1751 to correct an error in the Julian calendar was not adopted by Russia until 1918. Old-style dates were 13 days behind new-style ones. In this book I have used old-style dates for events in Russia before 1918.

Everyone was taken by surprise by the events which took place at the end of February 1917. It will help us if we take each day as it happened:

18 February A strike broke out among the steel-workers at the Petilov works in Petrograd. By 21 February the strike had spread to other industrial plants. N.H. Sukhanov took an active part in the later stages of the uprising. In his *Personal Record* he writes:

> In my office two typists were gossiping about food difficulties, rows in the shopping queues, unrest among the women, an attempt to smash into a warehouse. 'Do you know,' suddenly declared one of these young ladies, 'if you ask me, it's the beginning of the Revolution.'

23 February There was rioting in the queues at bakers' shops because of the shortage of bread. The 200 000 men on strike joined in, so did the people celebrating International Women's Day. Demonstrators carried red flags and banners with slogans such as 'We want bread', 'Down with the war' and 'Down with the autocracy'. There were clashes between the police and rioters.

24 February Sukhanov's *Personal Record* tells us:

> . . . the movement swept over St Petersburg like a great flood . . . the centre crowded with workers . . . meetings in the main streets . . . dispersed by Cossacks . . . but without any energy . . . .
> Unexpectedly the Cossack units displayed special sympathy with the revolution at several points, when in direct conversations they emphasized their neutrality and sometimes showed a clear tendency to fraternize. And on Friday evening . . . elections were held in the factories for the Soviet of Workers' Deputies . . . .

The movement spread into the working-class suburbs. Men from the districts north of the River Neva decided to go into the centre of the city. The police blocked the bridges across the frozen river but the workers made their way across the ice. They were joined by striking civil servants, teachers, students and other members of the middle class. There were many clashes between the crowds and the police.

25 February Workers began to occupy their factories and the number of strikers increased. The crowds in the streets were larger; the police did not appear on the streets in some districts. When a mounted policeman tried to seize a red flag from a demonstrator, a Cossack trooper cut him down with his sabre. One old man recalled:

'I knew the revolution had started when a Cossack winked at me.'

On 25 February the Tsarina sent a telegram to her husband at his headquarters at Mogilev:

> This is a hooligan movement, young people run and shout that there is no bread, simply to create excitement, along with workers who prevent others from working. If the weather were very cold they would all probably stay at home. But all this will pass and become calm, if only the Duma will behave itself.

The Tsar sent a telegram to General Khabalov, Commander of the Petrograd Military District, ordering him to suppress all disturbances.

26 February Khabalov ordered the troops to clear the streets; shots were fired and 40 demonstrators were killed by machine gunners from the Volhynian Regiment. These tactics seemed to work; the demonstrators fled and the streets of the centre were relatively clear.

The Prime Minister, Golitsyn, issued an order in the evening which instructed the Duma to dissolve. The Duma's President, Rodzianko, sent a telegram to the Tsar:

> The situation is serious. There is anarchy in the capital. The government is paralyzed. It is necessary immediately to entrust a person who enjoys the confidence of the country with the formation of the government. Any delay is equivalent to death. I pray God that in this hour responsibility will not fall on the sovereign.

After reading this message the Tsar impatiently remarked to his Minister of the Court, Count Fredericks: 'This fat Rodzianko has written me some nonsense to which I will not even reply.'

27 February In spite of the Prime Minister's decree, the Duma remained in session. Another body was also formed from delegates from various Petrograd factories, offices and other places of work. This committee, or *soviet*, met in the Tauride Palace where the Duma was also meeting. During the night of 26-27 February the soldiers from the Volhynian Regiment decided that they were not going to obey the orders to shoot. On 27 February they, and members of other regiments, joined in the revolution. As Sukhanov recalled:

23 A workers' demonstration outside the Winter Palace in 1917. Inside the palace, the Duma was trying to get to grips with the problems of governing war-weary and revolutionary Russia.

I elbowed my way . . . to the rooms occupied by the Soviet . . . one after another the soldiers' delegates told of what was happening in their companies. 'We're from the Volhynian Regiment . . . the Pavlovsky . . . the Lithuanian . . . the Keksholm . . . the Sappers . . . the Chasseurs . . . the Finnish . . . the Grenadiers . . . .

The name of each of the magnificent regiments that had launched the Revolution was met with a storm of applause. 'We had a meeting . . . . They told us not to serve against the people any more, we're going to join with our brother-workers, all united, to defend the people's cause' . . . . 'Long live the Revolution' . . . .

The Prime Minister, Golitsyn, now issued an order signed by the Tsar, ordering the Duma to dissolve, but the Duma continued to meet in

defiance of the Tsar. Khabalov (p. 31) issued a declaration of martial law, but his staff could not produce the glue to stick up the notices. They were then scattered around the streets, blown in the wind, trampled underfoot by the thousands of demonstrators who seemed almost to be in holiday mood as soldiers mingled with civilians from all classes.

Late that night the Tsar's ministers met in the Admiralty building but had to disperse when the electricity failed. The ministers never met again.

28 February Early in the morning the Tsar left Mogilev by train for his palace at Tsarskoe Selo, about 15 miles from the capital, to join his wife and children, who had measles. His progress was slow. Early on the morning of 1 March he was still 100 miles from the capital, when he was told that revolutionaries were in control of the track ahead. He decided to return to Pskov, his northern army headquarters where, late at night, his generals forced him to realize that Russia was in a state of revolution. He first thought of asking the Duma to form a government while he remained on the throne as a constitutional monarch. Then he decided to abdicate in favour of his son, but later changed his mind because of the Tsarevich's weak condition.

2 March The Tsar signed a decree of abdication naming his brother Michael as his successor, but on 3 March Michael refused to accept the crown. Ex-Tsar Nicholas was a prisoner at Tsarskoe Selo while all over Russia crowds rejoiced at the end of the Romanov dynasty. As Pasternak's hero says in *Dr Zhivago*:

> Do you realise what an unheard of thing is happening? Just think of it. The whole of Russia has had its roof torn off and you and I and every one else are out in the open. And there is nobody to spy on us. We are free; it is real freedom . . . freedom beyond our expectations.

YOUNG HISTORIAN

A

1 Account for the heavy losses suffered by the Russians in 1914 and 1915. How did these losses affect opinion among (a) the army, (b) the peasants, (c) industrial workers, and (d) politicians opposed to the Tsarist government?

2 Write a brief account of the influence of Rasputin in Russian affairs 1914-16.

3 Explain the growing unrest in Russia showing why (a) industrial workers (b) housewives and (c) soldiers became restless.

4 Explain why some historians think that the events of 27 February were the most important for the Tsarist regime.

5 Write a paragraph on each of the following: Rodzianko; Khabalov; the Petrograd Soviet; army headquarters, Mogilev.

B

Write the letters which might have been sent by:
(a) a soldier at the front in 1916;
(b) the mother of a soldier complaining about conditions at home;
(c) someone complaining of the Tsarina's growing influence;
(d) someone in Petrograd on 27 February.

C

Write the headlines which might have appeared above newspaper reports on:
(a) the Russian victories in early August 1914;
(b) the heavy defeat at Tannenberg later in August 1914;
(c) the dismissal of Grand Duke Nicholas as Commander-in-Chief;
(d) rising prices of food;
(e) army desertion;
(f) the murder of Rasputin;
(g) food riots, 23 February 1917;
(h) the demonstration of 24 February 1917;
(i) the massacre of 26 February 1917;
(j) the army's decision to join the revolution, 27 February 1917;
(k) the abdication of the Tsar, 2 March 1917;
(l) the abdication of Grand Duke Michael, 3 March 1917.

D

1 Draw a series of graphs to show the way in which food prices rose between 1914 and 1917. Write a brief note explaining (a) why the rises took place and (b) how these increases affected the political situation.

2 Draw an illustration to go with one of the following titles:
(a) the Russian soldier at the front;
(b) unrest at home;
(c) the abdication of the Tsar.

THE OVERTHROW OF DEMOCRACY, OCTOBER 1917

THE GOVERNMENT AFTER THE TSAR

On 27 February when Sukhanov had been at the Tauride Palace (p. 31):

... Miliukov came into the room from Rodzianko's office. At the sight of our group he came straight over to our table; he had a triumphant look and a repressed smile on his lips. 'A decision has been reached', he said, 'we're taking power' . . . .

Grand-Duke Michael's abdication manifesto invested this government with 'full powers' to hold office provisionally until the election of a Constituent Assembly which would draw up a constitution and work out a form of government. The Prime Minister was Prince Lvov (p. 29); Miliukov, leader of the Kadets (p. 20), was Foreign Minister, and the Minister of Justice was a left-wing Labourite, Kerensky (picture 24), the

24 Kerensky (second from the right) with some of his advisers. This picture was taken in October 1917, just before the Bolshevik Revolution.

34

son of Lenin's former schoolmaster (p. 10). Miliukov accepted, as successor to the Tsar, the treaty obligations of the old regime. The Provisional Government pledged 'the full honouring of our obligations towards our Allies'. This decision to continue with the war was to prove a major mistake on the part of the government.

DUAL GOVERNMENT

In another wing of the Palace were the 3 000 or so delegates of the Petrograd Soviet of Workers and Soldiers (picture 25). Here the SRP (p. 11), Mensheviks and a small number of Bolsheviks made their noisy ways in and out of the vast halls, eager to play their part in history-making. Should they co-operate with the Provisional Government? At first they decided not to — although Kerensky, a member of the Soviet, ignored the ban and accepted a leading post in the government. He was less hidebound than the Marxists who believed that *their* revolution — that of the working class — could not take place until the middle class had played their part in history. Once this had happened, then, inevit-

25   March 1917: a meeting of the Petrograd Soviet of Workers and Soldiers. The frequent elections in factories and military units meant that there was a constant flow of newcomers into the Soviet. However, it gradually came under the influence of the Bolsheviks.

ably according to Marxist teaching, the working class revolution would occur. The Soviet decided that it would supervise the work of the Provisional Government and issued a number of Orders or Decrees explaining their own and government policy to the people of Russia. Order Number 1 was issued in March and asked soldiers and sailors to form their own soviets, to control the arms and equipment, and to refuse to salute officers or stand to attention when talking to them. Most of the soldiers and sailors had been peasants in peacetime and were used to electing delegates to the village commune, or mir (p. 6). The idea of having their own commune, committee or soviet was nothing new to them.

The Petrograd workers as well as soldiers and sailors tended to disregard the decrees of the Provisional Government, looking to their own elected representatives in the Soviet for a lead. 'Who elected you?' roared one Soviet delegate, to the frightened members of the Provisional Government.

AT THE FRONT

26   Soldiers at the front welcoming the news of the February Revolution, 1917.

With many soldiers busy playing at politics, others eager to get home to take part in land redistribution, most refusing to accept any discipline and many openly deserting (picture 20), the Russian army began to fall to pieces. Officers who tried to force the men to fight were shot or sometimes lynched. Sailors at the naval base at Kronstadt killed an admiral and 50 other officers.

THE LAND PROBLEM

Trotsky had spoken of the close link between the conscript army and the Russian peasant (p. 29). This link became closer as millions of deserting soldiers made their way home, carrying with them the revolutionary ideas they had picked up at the front. Right across Russia there were lootings, burnings and lynchings as peasants drove landlords from their estate. This only made the peasant soldiers all the more anxious to get home in case all the land would have gone before they had returned. The number of estates seized rose from 17 in March, 204 in April, 259 in May, 577 in June to 1,122 in July. However,

the Provisional Government contented itself with setting up a Commission 'to look into the land question' while affirming that no changes could be considered until the war had been won.

THE INDUSTRIAL WORKERS

Life in the industrial towns was chaotic. John Reed, an American journalist, reported:

> Under dull grey skies, in the shortening days, the rain fell drenching, incessant. The mud underfoot was deep, slippery and clinging, worse than usual because of the complete breakdown of municipal administration . . . . The streets were dark and robberies and housebreaking increased. Men took turns at all-night guard duty with loaded rifles . . . . Food queues began to assemble before dawn.

Workers came out on strike to demand better pay because of the ever-rising prices; they asked for, and in May obtained, an eight-hour day. Many of them occupied the factories, elected their soviets and their delegates to the Petrograd Soviet and to the Congress of All-Russian

Soviets which had its headquarters in the Smolny Institute which had been a girls' boarding school. The workers were determined that, whatever happened at the Tauride Palace, the capitalist bosses would not regain their industrial power. The revolution had not been fought for the capitalists.

LENIN BACK TO RUSSIA

Lenin was in Switzerland when the February revolution started. By the end of March the Germans were anxious that the Russians should pull out of the war. To ensure that this happened they provided a train in which Lenin travelled across Germany into Sweden. From here Lenin and his wife crossed into Finland in small Finnish sledges, took another train and arrived at the Finland Station in Petrograd on 3 April. He was met by a great crowd led by the Menshevik chairman of the Petrograd Soviet. Lenin ignored him and spoke to the crowd. An eye-witness recalled Lenin's speech:

> the workers and soldiers had heroically over-thrown the autocracy and had, within a few days, turned Russia from a politically backward country into one of the freest democratic states. 'And now they want to palm off on us another tsar — capital. But the factories and mills must belong not to the capitalists but to you, and the land must not belong to the landowners but to the peasants. Long live the socialist revolution!' It seemed as though the workers and soldiers were spellbound. They were not used to hearing such words. Then they broke their silence and applauded and cheered . . . .

Lenin set to work to inspire his Bolshevik supporters. On 7 April in the Bolshevik newspaper *Pravda* he published the views which have become known as his 'April Theses'. The main points of his article were that the Bolsheviks should no longer support the Provisional Government, but ought to try to create a Republic of workers' and peasants' Soviets; 'All power to the soviets' should be the slogan. He wanted the nationalization of all land, workers' control of all factories and farms and, above all, an end to the war. Within a week most of the Bolsheviks accepted his view.

MORE UNREST, APRIL-MAY

Under Lenin's directions the Bolsheviks now went to work among the soldiers and workers. They convinced the members of the Petrograd garrison that only the Bolsheviks would bring peace, so ensuring that in the event of a struggle with the government the soldiers would at least remain neutral and might even come out in support of Lenin. They also set out to train their own Red Guard of armed workmen who would play an important part if there were a struggle with the government. Lenin was not prepared to play a waiting, Marxist, game. He said, 'Power is not given up, it is taken by force.'

In the more militant suburbs of the capital his agents raised two slogans: 'Down with the ten capitalist ministers' and 'All power to the soviets'. The first slogan was intended to rouse the rank and file against the middle class Kadets and, as did also the second slogan, to appeal to Mensheviks and other radicals. Indeed it was the Menshevik-dominated Soviet which organized vast processions of up to 500 000 workers and soldiers who roared through the streets of the capital carrying the Bolshevik slogans. Even though Lenin did not yet have a majority among the delegates at the Soviet he was on his way to winning popular support which would later be translated into a Bolshevik-dominated Soviet.

On 19 and 20 April soldiers and sailors marched to arrest the Provisional Government because of its determination to continue the war. Moderate Soviet delegates were sent to calm them down and managed to get them to return to their barracks. This and another mass demonstration on 22 April led to a government reshuffle in which Kerensky, the left-wing Labourite, became Minister for War. He went to the front to try to rouse the soldiers for one more great effort against Germany.

A major war offensive was launched under Brusilov in June 1917. At first there were small victories but by 2 July the commander was reporting a defeat and losses of 40 000 men. These were small losses compared to the massive losses of 1915 and 1916. But, though small, they were the last straw. The army began to retreat of its own accord; retreat turned into panic, the frightened soldiers looting as they went, murdering their officers and assaulting women and children.

27   One of many posters produced to remind the Russian people that Lenin was their great leader.

THE JULY DAYS

The news of the defeat brought the Petrograd workers onto the streets. Armed mobs of soldiers, sailors and workers, smashed shop windows, and broke into private houses, looting and killing as they went. They laid siege to the Tauride Palace where they tried to force the Soviet to take over the government. Chernov, the SRP Minister of Agriculture in the Provisional Government, was greeted with the cry: 'Take power when you're offered it, you son of a bitch.' But he and his colleagues on the Soviet Executive Committee were unwilling to take power at the request of an unruly mob. They preferred to wait for organized elections. Even

the Bolsheviks were booed for refusing to take an active role. Lenin wanted to wait 'until the apple is ripe' before he moved against the government. The workers did not understand this and took his refusal to act as the decision of a coward. On the other hand the government blamed Lenin and the Bolsheviks for having roused the workers with their propaganda (picture 27). When the rioters returned to home and work on 5 July, troops loyal to the government drove the Bolsheviks from their headquarters and closed down the offices of *Pravda*. Some leaders, including Trotsky, were arrested. Lenin went into hiding, shaving off his beard and wearing a wig.

28   The scene outside the Duma building in July 1917, when the Bolsheviks rose in rebellion, besieged the Duma but were dispersed by troops loyal to the Provisional Government.

29 General Kornilov, speaking to Russian soldiers in July 1917. He persuaded them to continue to fight against the Germans. The failure of the June 1917 offensive increased the unpopularity of Kerensky's government. Kornilov tried to seize power to set up a military dictatorship, but failed.

THE KORNILOV AFFAIR

One result of the July riots was a change of government, Kerensky becoming Prime Minister on 8 July. He failed to follow up his success — and did not hunt down Lenin and the other Bolsheviks, whose organization remained intact. He also decided to ignore the land problem and to get on with waging the war.

The partial victory over the forces of the left encouraged some generals to try and restore some discipline in the army and navy. The new Commander-in-Chief, General Kornilov (picture 29), claimed that when he had done this, he would march on Petrograd to destroy the

talking about the inevitability of their being brought to power by popular votes — first in the soviets, then, when elections were held for the Constituent Assembly, through that government-making body.

On 7 October Lenin returned secretly from Finland and took his place on the Central Committee of the Bolshevik Party. He used his energy to persuade his colleagues that they ought not to wait longer for power but ought to seize it by force. On 10 October the decision was taken; there would be an armed uprising and a seizure of power, although no date was fixed.

Trotsky organized the Red Guards (picture 30) and managed to acquire machine guns and rifles. He obtained a vast store of munitions by winning the support of the troops in the Peter and Paul Fortress in the heart of the capital, from which artillery might be used to bombard the Provisional Government in the Tauride Palace. In October the Bolshevik-led Petrograd Soviet set up a Military Revolutionary Committee through which Trotsky was able to influence the soldiers in other garrisons in Petrograd.

Kerensky seemed unable to decide what to do. On 25 September he formed a new government with Socialist and non-Socialist members. He continued to believe that the war had to be fought and that, having overthrown an autocratic government, he was bound to allow the maximum amount of freedom in the new Republic. Lenin and the Bolsheviks used this freedom to draw attention to the government's failures and to urge the people to follow the Bolshevik line of 'Peace by your own feet' and 'Land by your own hand'.

On 23 October Kerensky decided to take action against the Bolsheviks. But by this time few troops in the capital were willing to obey the government's orders. He was forced to bring loyal troops back from the front and to use young officer cadets to close down the Bolshevik newspapers and to raise the bridges across the River Neva so that the working class suburbs would be cut off from the city centre. Orders were given for the cruiser *Aurora* to sail from her anchorage in the Neva and put to sea — for fear that the sailors might support the Bolsheviks.

But all of this was in vain. Bolshevik workmen

Bolsheviks. Kerensky appeared to encourage him, but once the march had started Kerensky realized that Kornilov, a right-wing, old-fashioned general, might use his power to turn on the government and establish himself as a Tsarist dictator. On 27 August he dismissed Kornilov from his post. Kornilov continued his march towards Petrograd. Kerensky appealed to the Bolshevik-led workers. They came onto the streets to defend their capital and their revolution. But they did not have to fight. Many of Kornilov's troops deserted as they neared the city while the railwaymen switched the trains carrying the army into sidings or branch lines so that Kornilov never reached Petrograd.

BOLSHEVIK POPULARITY

The Bolsheviks became increasingly popular; they had, it seemed, defeated Kornilov; they wrote, and spoke continually of the need for a solution to the land problem and an end to the unpopular war. Early in September Kerensky released the Bolsheviks who had been imprisoned in July (p. 38). Trotsky took part in new elections to the soviets and, for the first time, there were Bolshevik majorities in the soviets in Petrograd, Moscow and other cities. On 25 September Trotsky became Chairman of the Petrograd Soviet. With Lenin still in hiding, in Finland, the majority of the Bolsheviks were lowered the bridges across the Neva; the *Aurora* sailed away only to anchor again a mere mile down river, Bolshevik newspapers continued to be printed. The Bolshevik Central Committee was in almost continual session, debating whether or not to rise and take power by force. Finally, at four o'clock in the morning of 25 October one of them told John Reed:

> We are moving; we've pinched the Minister for Justice and the Minister for Religion .... One regiment is on the march to capture the telephone exchange, another the telegraphic agency, another the State Bank. The Red Guard is out.

The Bolshevik forces met little resistance. Inside the Tauride Palace the members of the government were blockaded by Bolshevik forces. These were so unsure of what was happening that they saluted Prime Minister Kerensky as he left to go to the front to try to raise loyal troops. It was late evening before the Bolsheviks demanded the surrender of the government which was defended by a few Cossacks, some young cadets and a Women's Battalion of Death

(picture 31). The government refused to surrender. The Cossacks deserted their posts, the Bolsheviks slipped into the Palace, the cadets surrendered and, though the women were prepared to fight, they were persuaded that it would be futile. At nine o'clock the great guns of the *Aurora* boomed out as did the artillery of the Peter and Paul Fortress. At midnight the Bolshevik forces stormed the almost deserted Palace and arrested the ministers there.

THE CONGRESS OF SOVIETS

At eleven o'clock in the evening of 25 October the All-Russian Congress of Soviets came together for its second Congress. There were about 650 delegates of whom 390 were Bolsheviks who had the support of the Left SRP. The Mensheviks and right-wing members of the SRP condemned the Bolsheviks' use of force against the Provisional Government but they were answered by Trotsky, when he declared:

> What do they offer us? .... To give up our victory, to compromise, and to negotiate — with whom? With whom shall we negotiate? With those miserable cliques which have left

31   A women's battalion standing at ease during the October Revolution, 1917.

32 Some of the Bolshevik leaders together during the October Revolution. Trotsky, in peaked cap and light uniform, was then a more important person than Stalin, on the extreme right of the picture.

the Congress or with those who still remain? But we saw how strong those cliques were! There is no one left in Russia to follow them. And millions of workers and peasants are asked to negotiate with them on equal terms. No, an agreement will not do now. To those who have left us and to those proposing negotiations we must say: You are a mere handful, miserable, bankrupt; your role is finished, and you may go where you belong — to the garbage heap of history.

On the next day the Congress cheered Lenin on his first appearance and entrusted the power of government to the exclusively Bolshevik Council of 15 People's Commissars. The Congress also passed two important decrees. One was to seek peace with Germany and Austria. The other nationalized all land 'to be made freely available to those prepared to cultivate it with their own labour', which, on the surface, appeared to give the peasants possession of their land.

The Bolsheviks seized power in Moscow after some heavy fighting but elsewhere there was chaos. It would require a great deal of fighting in a savage Civil War before Bolshevik government controlled the whole of Russia (pp.45-52).

THE CONSTITUENT ASSEMBLY

During the autumn — after the Bolsheviks seized power — elections were held for the Constituent Assembly. In this, the only free election ever to take place in Russia, the Bolsheviks won only a quarter of the votes, the majority (over 60 per cent) going to the moderate Socialists who hoped that Lenin would hand over power to this Assembly when it met on 5

33. Red Guards in action during the October Revolution, 1917.

January 1918. At the first meeting a Socialist tried to start the proceedings but Lenin's colleague, Sverdlov, insisted on reading a declaration of Bolshevik policy and asked the Assembly to approve it. When the majority refused, the Bolsheviks walked out, to the cheers of the Bolshevik-led soldiers, sailors and workers crowding the public gallery. The Assembly continued to debate throughout the day and night until, at five o'clock the following morning, a sailor-guard ordered the delegates to leave because the guard wanted to go home. On the following day Lenin's Soviet Executive Committee dissolved the Assembly and it never met again. Democracy had a short life in Russia, whose capital city was to be renamed Leningrad in honour of the organizer of the October Revolution.

YOUNG HISTORIAN

A

1 Explain the significance of the part played in 1917 by the Petrograd Soviet. Why did it fall under Bolshevik control in the summer of 1917?

2 How far was the Provisional Government to blame for its own downfall? Can you suggest what steps it might have taken which might have ensured its success?

3 Explain the importance of Lenin's April Theses.

4 Show how the Bolsheviks prepared the ground for their eventual seizure of power. Do you think that they might have been prevented from gaining power?

5 Explain the importance of each of the following in shaping events in Russia: the Brusilov campaign; the July riots; the Kornilov affair.

6 What was the significance of the part played by Trotsky in 1917?

7 Explain why Kerensky fell from power and why Lenin was able to seize it.

8 Write a paragraph on each of the following: the All-Russian Congress of Soviets; the *Aurora*; *Pravda*; the Constituent Assembly.

B

1 Write the letter which might have been sent by a supporter of Miliukov explaining his determination to continue with the war.

2 Write the letter which a soldier might have sent explaining why he and many of his colleagues were anxious that the war should end.

3 Write the letters which might have been sent by (a) a soldier and (b) an officer after reading Order Number 1 from the Petrograd Soviet.

4 Write the letter which a peasant mother might have sent to her soldier son about the seizure of estates which took place throughout 1917.

5 Write the letter which a non-Bolshevik might have sent from Petrograd after the July riots.

C

Write the headlines which might have appeared above newspaper reports on:
(a) the formation of the Provisional Government, March 1917;
(b) the appearance of Order Number 1 of the Petrograd Soviet;
(c) the seizure of an estate — in a local newspaper;
(d) Lenin's return;
(e) the April demonstrations;
(f) the failure of the Brusilov campaign;
(g) Trotsky's arrest;
(h) Kornilov's march;
(i) Kornilov's failure;
(j) the election of Trotsky as Chairman of the Petrograd Soviet;
(k) the sailing of the *Aurora*;
(l) the Bolshevik rising of 25 October;
(m) Trotsky's 'garbage heap' speech;
(n) the dissolution of the Constituent Assembly.

43

LENIN IN POWER, 1918-1924

RUSSIA'S POLITICAL PROBLEMS, 1918

Lenin's overthrow of the Provisional Government had been opposed by the Mensheviks and some members of the SRP in the Petrograd Soviet. The dismissal of the Constituent Assembly was seen by opponents, as well as by Bolsheviks, as the death of democracy. As Trotsky said, 'The simple, open, brutal breaking up of the Constituent Assembly, dealt formal democracy a stroke from which it has never recovered.' The politicians who had looked forward to the creation of a democratic form of government were angered by the Bolsheviks' action. Some members of the SRP set up their own form of government — in eastern and northern Russia. Others supported the uprisings by ex-Tsarist generals who plunged Russia into a long period of bitter and devastating civil war (p. 46).

Between January and July 1918 the Congress of Soviets considered Bolshevik proposals for a new form of government for Russia. The debates were bitter as Lenin's opponents accused the Bolsheviks of being intent on creating a new form of autocracy. In July the Congress agreed the constitution which created the Russian Socialist Federal Soviet Republic (RSFSR) which gave supreme power to the All-Russian Congress of Soviets. Delegates to this Congress were elected in town and rural constituencies. In towns there was one delegate for every 25 000 people; in the rural areas one delegate represented 125 000 people, so that the industrial workers were over-represented, which suited the Bolsheviks. This Congress had to elect an executive committee of about 200 people which in turn appointed the Council of People's Commissars;

this latter was dominated by the Central Politburo of the Bolshevik Party which had its own inner circle of about five members who were dominated by Lenin. Lenin knew that he was creating a dictatorship — but argued:

> The Soviet Socialist Democracy is in no way inconsistent with the rule and dictatorship of one person; the will of a class is at times best realized by a dictator who sometimes can accomplish more by himself.

THE ECONOMY

The political unrest took place against a background of continuing and worsening economic dislocation. Peasants continued to riot in the country and food continued to be in short supply in the industrial towns; transport continued to be chaotic as roving bands of soldiers seized sections of railway track, and anarchists and bandits pulled up lines or stripped away signalling equipment. Prices continued to rise while workers looked forward in vain to the dawn of the days of plenty which they had been promised would follow the revolution. The loss of the Ukraine (p. 46), Russia's granary, added to the economic and social unrest.

Lenin had a third problem to face. He had promised the Russians that he would make peace. Many Russians were opposed to this. The SRP and Mensheviks had continued with the war after February 1917; they were unwilling to accept Lenin's peace proposals in January 1918. The ex-Tsarist officers and Russian patriots, as well as some of Lenin's own Bolsheviks, were equally opposed to submitting to the Germans. Russia's Western Allies — Britain, France and the USA as well as Japan, were all angry at the news that Lenin was seeking to make peace. They sent in troops, supplies and money to support the anti-Bolsheviks and so added to the turmoil of the civil war (p. 46).

34 Counter-revolutionary forces and foreign intervention.

THE TREATY OF BREST-LITOVSK, 1918

Lenin's government issued a large number of decrees or laws in the early months of 1918. Education was to be free; everyone was to be covered by a system of national insurance which would provide pensions, a health service and assistance for the unemployed; all ranks and titles were abolished and a campaign mounted

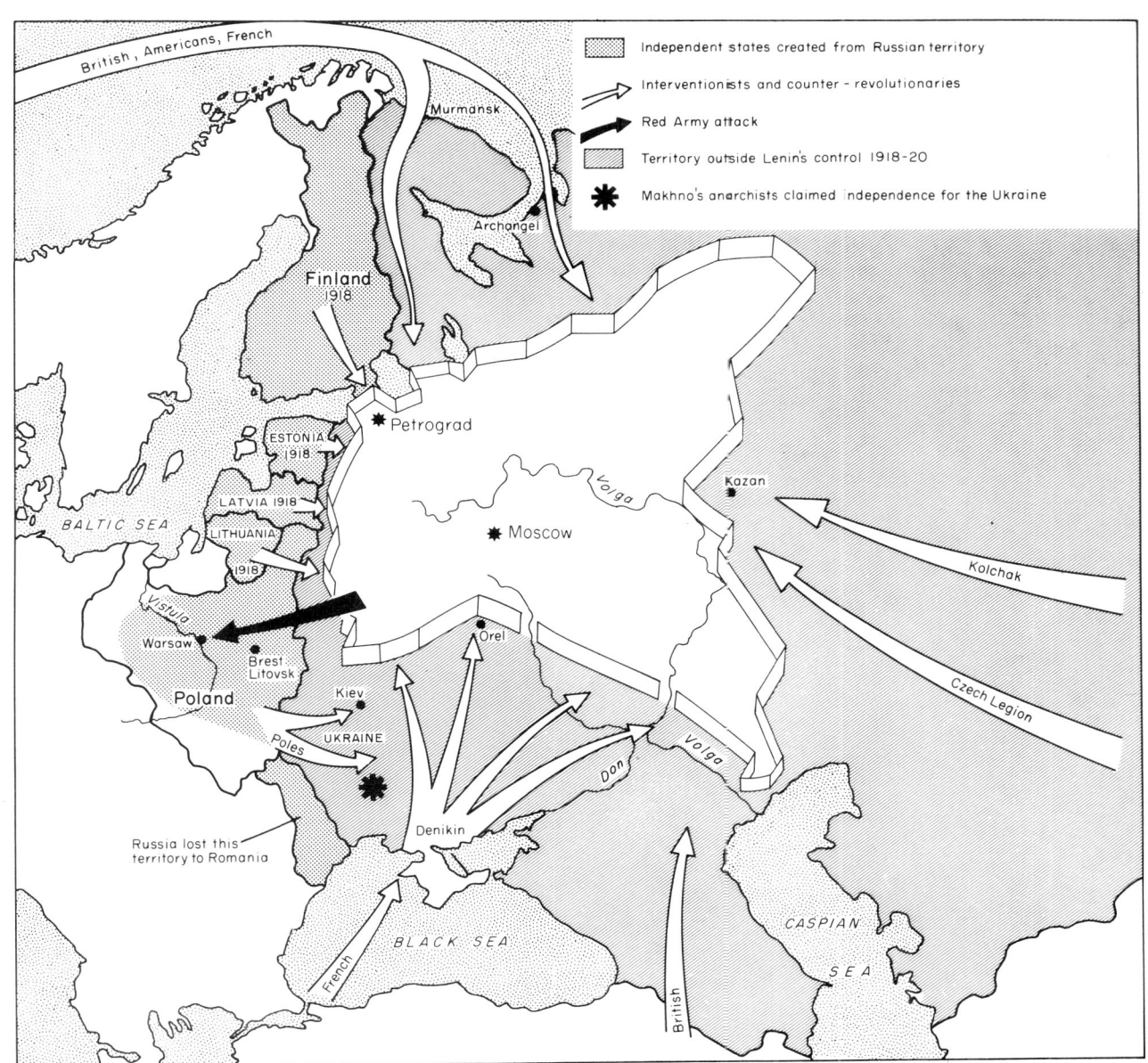

Independent states created from Russian territory

Interventionists and counter - revolutionaries

Red Army attack

Territory outside Lenin's control 1918-20

Makhno's anarchists claimed independence for the Ukraine

British, Americans, French

Murmansk

Archangel

Finland 1918

Petrograd

ESTONIA 1918

LATVIA 1918

LITHUANIA 1918

BALTIC SEA

Volga

Kazan

Moscow

Kolchak

Czech Legion

Vistula

Warsaw

Brest Litovsk

Poland

Orel

Kiev

Poles

UKRAINE

Don

Volga

Russia lost this territory to Romania

Denikin

French

BLACK SEA

British

CASPIAN SEA

against adult illiteracy. The government also changed the calendar to bring it in line with the Western calendar and, as another sign of change, the capital was shifted from Petrograd to Moscow — a safer city than the old capital, much further away from German troops.

While this reforming spate was rushing along, Lenin arranged an armistice with the Germans in December and Trotsky was sent to negotiate peace terms with the Germans. The negotiations in the Polish town of Brest-Litovsk lasted until March, with the Russians behaving as though they had won (picture 34). They were waiting for that long-talked-of world revolution.

When the Germans refused to accept Russian proposals, Trotsky countered by refusing German proposals and returning to Petrograd. The German army then advanced — as it might have done at any time. The Russians were then forced to accept a set of much harsher terms.

In the Treaty of Brest-Litovsk the Russians lost Poland, Finland, the Baltic States of Estonia, Latvia and Lithuania and, perhaps most important of all, the Ukraine, which became independent. One third of European Russia was lost. The loss of the food producing areas was a great disaster; so, too, were the losses of one-third of all Russia's ironworks, three-quarters of all her coal deposits and one-third of her population.

Many Bolsheviks and even more non-Bolshevik members of the Soviets accused Lenin of being a traitor for having signed away so much of Russian land and wealth. But he got them to vote for the peace terms:

Our impulse tells us to rebel, to refuse to sign this robber peace. Our reason will in our calmer moments tell us the plain naked truth — that Russia can offer no physical resistance because she is materially exhausted by a three-years' war . . . . The Russian Revolution must sign the peace to obtain a breathing space to recuperate for the struggle. The central point of the world struggle now is the rivalry between English and German finance-capital. Let the Revolution utilize this struggle for its own ends.

THE CREATION OF THE DICTATORSHIP

The constitution which was hammered out by July 1918 had put all power into the hands of a
46

small number of Commissars. The majority of political activists were opposed to this development. They tried to carry their opposition before the people, using, as Lenin had done after April 1917, the press and public meetings to do so. Lenin put a stop to their activities when he signed a decree on the Press:

The bourgeois press is one of the mighty weapons of the bourgeoisie. When the new Workers' and Peasants' Government is just getting started, it is not possible to leave in the hands of the enemy a weapon no less dangerous than bombs and machine-guns . . . .

The Soviet of the People's Commissars decrees that:

1. Those organs of the press will be closed which (a) call for open opposition to the Workers' and Peasants' Government; (b) sow sedition by a frankly slanderous perversion of facts . . . (c) encourage deeds of a manifestly criminal character . . . .

Lenin then set up the All-Russian Extraordinary Commission for Fighting Counter Revolution which from its initials was known as the Cheka. This was a secret police force which functioned much as had the secret police of the Tsarist regime. The Cheka initiated a period of Red Terror; people were seized, tortured, imprisoned without trial, executed or interned in concentration camps. Lenin used the Cheka first against the Kadets or Liberals; then he turned on the non-Bolshevik Socialists — Mensheviks and members of the SRP. Later he used it against members of his own party, especially after the Tenth Party Congress of March 1921 had imposed a ban on all opposition by groups within the Communist Party. Those few Bolsheviks who might have wished to oppose this last turn of the dictator's screw were powerless after having combined with him to deprive all other parties of power and freedom. In Tsarist days men had spoken hopefully of the capping of the pyramid (p. 7). Lenin alone capped the pyramid after 1920 (picture 27).

THE CIVIL WAR

The news of the Treaty of Brest-Litovsk was merely one more reason why many opposed Lenin. For various reasons a variety of men appealed to the Russian people for support in a struggle against the new dictator-Tsar. From the east came news of the rampaging of the Czech prisoners-of-war. These had been members of the Austrian army and had been captured during the Russian successes in and after 1914. By 1917 the Allies had succeeded in persuading them to form themselves into a pro-Allied and anti-Austrian force which would help defeat the Central Powers and so play a part in the setting up of a new, independent Czechoslovakia. They had been on their way to Vladivostok from where they were going to sail to western Europe and take the side of the Allies. Once Russia had made peace with Germany this plan was cancelled and the Czechs were then left to make their own long way home. Trotsky, now Commissar for War, had to organize a peasant army to put them down. Meanwhile, in Siberia, Admiral Kolchak raised the flag of revolt against the upstart Lenin. Better the Provisional Government (p. 34-35) or, indeed, the restoration of the Tsar, than government by a self-imposed dictator. The Tsar and his family were taken prisoners in the village of Ekaterinburg which lay on the route being taken by Kolchak's forces on their way to Moscow (picture 35). The Cheka then killed them so that the rebels, or Whites, as they were called, might not have a monarch around whom to rally.

From the north came the army led by ex-General Yudenich. Based on Estonia this force came within sight of Petrograd at one point before being defeated. From the Crimea there were revolts led first by Denikin and later by Baron Wrangel whose forces made their way through southern Russia and seemed likely to capture Moscow. From the Ukraine came the peasants' army led by the brilliant Anarchist, Makhno, who wanted independence for that province. From Turkestan came rebels financed and aided by the British. These captured Baku and control of the oil-bearing region of Turkestan.

The British were not the only foreigners who intervened. Allied anger at Russian withdrawal was increased by the news that the Russian government would not repay the loans made to

35 The Tsar and his family at Tobolsk, where they were interned from September 1917 to April 1918.

36 British troops on duty in northern Russia, 1919.

the Tsarist government (p. 8). The Allies were also concerned about the large dumps of arms which they had sent to Russia and which might fall into German hands. So Britain sent forces to Archangel and Murmansk (picture 36) to guard the arms dumps and help the northern rebels in the hope that a new, more co-operative government might be set up. France sent armies into Poland and into the Crimea to help the rebels there. American, British and Japanese forces aided the Kolchak forces and tried to help the Czechs.

If you look at picture 34, you can get some idea of the extent of the anti-Bolshevik movement and the number of separate groups taking part. It was a wonder that the Bolsheviks managed to win. That they did so was due in part to the Whites themselves who never formed a united front, fought their own battles for different things and never succeeded in winning the support of the Russian people. As Serge points out:

37   Troops of Kolchak's White Army shooting Bolshevik prisoners.

The White disaster was the result of two cardinal errors: their failure to have the intelligence and courage to carry out agrarian reform in the territories they wrested from the Revolution, and their reinstatement everywhere of the ancient trinity of generals, high clergy and landlords . . . .

On the other had the Reds were scarcely any more considerate of the peasants. In the name of War Communism, food was requisitioned and men forcibly conscripted into the army; looting and pillaging was as widescale on the Red side as on that of the Whites (picture 37). But the Reds did have a unified command which was dominated by Trotsky who showed great energy and skill. He had his armoured train in which he carried armoured cars, tanks, guns and other weapons and in which he rushed from front to front, bringing help where it was most needed.

The Reds also had much more convenient lines of communication than had the Whites. Based on Petrograd and Moscow the Reds were fighting from a compact 'inside' whereas the disunited Whites were attacking along a wide front,

their lines of communication being stretched ever further as they advanced towards the Bolshevik centres. Lenin used the Cheka ruthlessly against potential rebels inside his increasingly smaller camp and he also used the patriotic call when he appealed to the Russians to help him resist the attacks from the foreigners:

> Kolchak and Denikin are the chief enemies of the Soviet Republic. If it were not for the help they are getting from the Entente (England, France and America) they would have gone to pieces long ago .... The truth ... has now been fully revealed. Shooting of tens of thousands of workers ... flogging of peasants of entire districts. Public flogging of women .... Let every worker and peasant know ... what awaits him in the event of a victory for Kolchak or Denikin.

WAR COMMUNISM

The economic and social effects of the Civil War were widespread. The transport system became

38 A funeral for Bolshevik victims of the October Revolution, 1918. This demonstration of camaraderie among the Bolsheviks was really tested during the Civil War.

even more chaotic; food was in ever-increasing short supply; consumer goods even more so. Pasternak described Russia's condition in *Dr Zhivago*:

> .... He had followed the railway, all of it out of action .... Train after train ... stood idle, stopped by the defeat of Kolchak, by running out of fuel and by snowdrifts .... They stretched for miles on end ... fortresses for armed bands of robbers or hide-outs for escaping criminals ... mass graves of the victims of the cold and of the typhus ... mowing down whole villages ....

Lenin announced a policy known as War Communism which was described by Serge:

> 'War Communism' could be defined as follows: firstly, requisitioning in the countryside; secondly, strict rationing for the town population, who were classified into categories; thirdly, complete 'socialization' of production

49

and labour; fourthly, an extremely complicated and chit-ridden system of distribution for the remaining stocks of manufactured goods; fifthly, a monopoly of power tending towards the single Party and the suppression of all dissent; sixthly, a state of siege, and the Cheka. This system had been approved by the Ninth Congress of the Communist Party in the March and April of 1920 . . . .

Clashes between the peasants and the Commissars who were sent out to requisition the grain were frequent and bloody. The unemployed, who had no ration cards, were forced to become bandits and seek for food as best they might. In the towns and cities life took on a grim aspect; Serge remembered:

Towards the city centre, gentle ghost-like hints of life began. Open sleds, pulled by starving horses, proceeded unhurriedly over the white expanse. There were practically no cars. The rare passers-by, eaten by cold and hunger, had faces of ghastly white. Squads of half-ragged soldiers, their rifles often hanging from their shoulders by a rope, tramped around under the red pennants of their units . . . .

50

39 A view of the Smolensk Market in Moscow, in September 1921, after Lenin had allowed private traders to take an active part in Russian economic life.

The people of Russia were not willing to be communized. Lenin had to face the reality and in March 1921 he announced a change of policy when he introduced what has become known as the New Economic Policy. The peasants were not producing the amount of food required by the industrial workers and the army. Under the NEP the government took part of the peasants' crops at low prices but allowed the peasant to sell whatever he had left over on the free market for whatever he could get. NEP also allowed the setting up of small businesses in the industrial towns; Lenin hoped that the capitalist producers would provide a supply of consumer goods and so attract the peasant to sell his surplus food — to get the money to buy the consumer goods (picture 39). Many Bolsheviks and other socialists thought that this new policy was a return to private enterprise. Lenin declared:

The civil war of 1918-20 greatly increased the devastation of the country . . . . To this was added the failure of the harvest of 1920 . . . . We were forced to resort to 'War Communism'

... a temporary measure. We cannot give the peasant manufactured goods for all we require ... we are introducing the tax in kind, i.e. we shall take the minimum of grain we require for the army and the workers ... and will obtain the rest in exchange for manufactured goods .... We cannot hope to restore large-scale factory state socialist production at one stroke .... It is necessary to help to restore small industry ... the effect will be the revival of the petty bourgeoisie and of capitalism .... The proletarian regime is in no danger as long as the proletariat firmly hold ... transport and large-scale industry in its hands ....

UNREST

Many people came to the conclusion that Lenin's government was a failure. The workers in Petrograd and other centres came out on strike demanding the right to form unions, hold meetings, share in decision-making and higher wages. The Cheka and the Red Army were sent to put the leaders to death and drive the rest back to work. Even ardent Bolsheviks became disenchanted with the dictatorship, as Serge noted:

What with the political monopoly, the Cheka and the Red Army, all that now existed of the 'Commune-State' of our dreams was a theoretical myth. The war, the internal measures against counter-revolution, and the famine (which had created a bureaucratic rationing-apparatus) had killed off Soviet democracy. How could it revive, and when? The Party lived in the certain knowledge that the slightest relaxation of its authority would give the day to reaction.

During the winter of 1920-21 rations were cut in half; people in Petrograd burnt their furniture as fuel; clashes between peasants and Bolsheviks increased in number and savagery. But the greatest proof that there was a great deal that was wrong was the uprising which took place at the naval base at Kronstadt, the centre of the most fervent Bolshevik support in 1917 and 1918. In February 1921 the sailors rose in revolt against the treatment of the Petrograd strikers. They set up their own Soviet and issued a programme of which Serge writes:

It was a programme for the renewal of the Revolution. I will summarize it: re-election of the Soviets by secret ballot; freedom of the spoken and printed word for all revolutionary parties and groupings; freedom for the trade unions; the release of revolutionary political prisoners; abolition of official propaganda; an end to requisitioning in the countryside; freedom for the artisan class; immediate suppression of the barrier-squads that were stopping the people from getting their food as they pleased. The Soviet, the Kronstadt garrison, and the crews of the First and Second Naval

40 A Russian soldier-peasant at Lenin's funeral (1924), his eyes closed as he passes the bier on which Lenin's body is lying.

Squadrons were now in rebellion to ensure the triumph of this programme.

They talked of 'the Third Revolution' which would undo the damage of the Second (or October) Revolution. This uprising was brutally suppressed by Trotsky and his army, while the Cheka shot hundreds of prisoners who were captured at Kronstadt.

LENIN'S ILLNESS AND DEATH

In July 1918 a member of the SRP, Fanny Kaplan, had fired three shots at Lenin. He was seriously ill for a long time and although he recovered he was never fully fit again. The strains of the civil war, the need to impose himself continually on the less strong-willed members of the Politburo and the Council of Commissars, sapped his strength. The obvious unwillingness of the majority of Russians to accept what he thought was good for them and his inability to prevent the onset of a dreadful famine in 1921-22 even after the implementation of the NEP all told. Lenin had a stroke in 1922 and although he continued to rule Russia he was increasingly ineffective for two years before his death on 21 January 1924 (picture 40). He had overthrown Russia's first and only democratic Assembly, had instituted a dictatorship more rigorous and harsh than that of the Tsar and had failed to produce that paradise which he had promised his supporters. To his successors he left many problems. He also left them the instruments of dictatorship — control of the Press, a secret police with awesome powers and a grim record, a government dominated by whichever man could get to the top of the pyramid. We will see how these powers and instruments were used by Stalin.

YOUNG HISTORIAN

A

1 Explain why the Mensheviks and the SRP opposed Lenin after January 1918. Give three examples of ways in which Lenin tried to put an end to their opposition.

2 How did Lenin try to ensure that he had dictatorial powers in Russia after January 1918?

3 Give an account of the Treaty of Brest-Litovsk as it appeared to (a) a supporter of Lenin and (b) an opponent of the peace.

4 Examine the significance of (a) the decree on the Press (p. 46) and (b) the formation of the Cheka for (i) Lenin and (ii) his opponents.

5 Explain the reasons why the Civil War (a) was so widespread (b) lasted so long and (c) ended in a victory for the Reds.

6 Explain Lenin's reasons for introducing (a) War Communism and (b) NEP.

B

1 Write the letter which might have been sent by one of those who fought against Red rule after 1918.

2 Write the letter which might have been sent by an English soldier sent to fight against the Bolsheviks.

3 Write the letter which might have been sent from Petrograd during the winter of 1919-20 when there was a real danger of the city being captured by the British-supported General Yudenich.

4 Write the letter which a moderate might have sent after being at the Tenth Party Congress (p. 46).

C

Write the headlines which might have appeared above newspaper reports on:
(a) the publication of the decree on free education;
(b) the publication of the decree abolishing titles;
(c) the decision to make Moscow the capital of Russia;
(d) the signing of the Treaty of Brest-Litovsk;
(e) the publication of the decree on the Press;
(f) the establishment of the Cheka.

STALIN'S PRE-WAR YEARS, 1924-1939

STALIN'S EARLY CAREER

After the February Revolution, Stalin became editor of *Pravda*, the Bolshevik newspaper, and a member of the Military Revolutionary Committee which planned the details of the take-over in October 1917, when Lenin made him Chairman of the Commissariat for Nationalities. During the Civil War he organized the defence of Tsaritsyn (later named Stalingrad and now Volgograd) and was later sent with Dzerzhinsky, the head of the Cheka, to spur on the Red troops fighting against Kolchak (picture 37), following which he was appointed to take charge of the defence of Petrograd when it was threatened by Yudenich (p. 47).

AFTER THE CIVIL WAR

Stalin returned to his work at the Commissariat for Nationalities. His own state, Georgia, had declared itself independent during the Civil War. Stalin ordered a full-scale attack on the capital, Tiflis, in spite of Lenin's opposition. The rebels were put down in what has become known as 'The Rape of Georgia'. Lenin forgave the ruthless Stalin, promoted him to take charge of the Commissariat of Workers' and Peasants' Inspectorate. He also became head of Orgburo, which organized the growing Bolshevik Party, and, most important of all, he became General Secretary of the Central Committee of the Bolshevik Party which put him in touch with all the Party officials in the provinces. He was able to do little favours for them — and help them get promotion or favourable notices in the Press. In return they rigged elections to the Central Committee and Party Congresses in favour of Stalin's supporters. In this way Stalin gradually built up widespread and strong support inside the Party machine.

LENIN'S WARNING

Lenin saw the way in which Stalin had gained a powerful position. In his *Testament*, the dying Lenin wrote:

Comrade Stalin, having become General Secretary, has concentrated boundless authority in his hands, and I am not sure whether he will always be capable of using that authority with sufficient caution . . . . Stalin is too rude, and this defect, although quite tolerable in our midst and in dealings among us Communists, becomes intolerable in a General Secretary. That is why I suggested that the comrades think about a way of removing Stalin from that post and appointing somebody else differing in all other respects from Comrade Stalin solely in the degree of being more tolerant, more loyal, more polite and more considerate to the comrades, less capricious etc.

Stalin persuaded Trotsky, the most important leader after Lenin, not to publish this far-seeing document.

Lenin died on 21 January 1924 (picture 40). Stalin took charge of the arrangements and made the funeral oration which allowed him to appear to be Lenin's heir.

TROTSKY

Trotsky was easily the most intelligent of the small group around Lenin. He had travelled widely, written a large number of outstanding books, led the Petrograd Soviet in 1905 (p. 20) and organized the Red Army during the Civil War (p. 48). But many Bolsheviks were frightened by his obvious intelligence. They would have preferred someone more ordinary. They were also aware of the fact that he had only joined the Bolsheviks in 1917, having been a Menshevik until then. Was this late-comer to be trusted with the leadership?

Even while Lenin was still alive, Trotsky advocated a relaxation of party discipline to allow free discussion on the problems facing Russia. Stalin reminded the 12th Party Congress that this was contrary to the Leninist doctrine that there should be no opposition even inside the Party (p. 46). When Trotsky went on to call for a war against the peasants as a way of solving the shortage of grain and the rising food prices, it was Stalin who argued that Lenin's NEP policy called for co-operation with the peasants. Trotsky tried to rouse the Congress to adopt a crash programme of industrialization:

> Moscow is the capital of the Communist International. You travel a few scores of kilometres and — there is wilderness, snow and fir and frozen mud and wild beasts . . . . Where Shatura [power] station stands, elks roamed a few years ago. Now metal pylons of exquisite construction run the whole way down from Moscow.

But Stalin spoke the language which the ordinary Party delegate understood: '. . . the power station would be of no more use to Russia than a gramophone was to a peasant who did not possess even a cow.'

THE ANTI-TROTSKY STRUGGLE

Stalin was not in fact the most important member of the anti-Trotsky group inside the government and Party. Zinoviev who ran the party in Leningrad, and Kamenev who was Party boss in Moscow, were his seniors. It was Zinoviev and Kamenev who were most opposed to Trotsky's belief in world revolution and who wanted 'Socialism in One Country'. Trotsky's call for more speedy industrialization and a war against the peasants was defeated at the 13th Party Congress in May 1924.

Trotsky then made another serious mistake. In a book, *The Lessons of October*, he showed how Zinoviev and Kamenev had opposed Lenin's call for an uprising in October 1917. This angered the two party bosses who allied themselves with Stalin at the 14th Party Congress in December 1925, which dismissed Trotsky from his post as Commissar for War. Stalin had packed the Congress with his provincial supporters (p. 53) so that Trotsky, once the darling of the crowd, hardly got a hearing.

THE ATTACK ON ZINOVIEV AND KAMENEV

The leaders of the big city parties now tried to use their power to make life easier for their supporters — the industrial workers. Under the NEP unemployment was rising, the workers went hungry, but the peasants prospered. The workers demanded a change. They wanted more investment in industry and more government control over food prices. Stalin denounced this as Trotskyism and anti-Leninism. He turned to the other members of the Politburo for support. Bukharin, Rykov and Tomsky sided with Stalin against Zinoviev and Kamenev; the Party Congress denounced the two city bosses for the very crime of which they had accused Trotsky — intra-party fractionalism. Stalin's supporters, Kirov (picture 41) and Molotov took over in Leningrad and Moscow.

At the 15th Party Congress, Trotsky, Zinoviev and Kamenev joined forces against Stalin and demanded an all-out war against the peasants, a crash programme of industrialization and an end to the NEP which was producing only a larger middle class and a prosperous peasantry. However, Stalin's friends had produced a Congress which cheered him, jeered the opposition and expelled Trotsky from the Politburo and the Central Committee of the Party. In November 1927, on the tenth anniversary of Lenin's revolution, Trotsky tried to overthrow Stalin, but the Moscow crowds merely watched the procession of his followers through the streets; they

41   Kirov (on the left of the picture), Stalin (centre) and Voroshilov, sailing down the White Sea-Baltic Canal. This canal was one of the first of the major undertakings of the Bolshevik government.

did not follow as they had done in 1905 and as they had followed Lenin in 1917. Stalin then announced that Trotsky was being exiled to the Chinese frontier. He was deported in 1929 by which time Zinoviev and Kamenev had apologized and been brought back into the Party fold — to be used against Bukharin and his supporters when Stalin adopted Trotsky's policies of industrialization and war on the peasants in 1929.

STALIN AND INDUSTRIALIZATION

By 1928 Russia had made some progress along the road to industrialization in spite of the heavy losses suffered in the Treaty of Brest-Litovsk (p. 45). But Russia was still backward compared to the anti-Bolshevik Western capitalist countries. In 1928 Stalin launched the first Five-Year Plan:

We must transform the USSR from a weak, agrarian country dependent upon the caprices of world capitalism . . . drive out without mercy the capitalist elements, widen the front of the Socialist forms of economy, create the economic basis for the abolition of classes in the USSR and for the construction of a Socialist society . . . create in our country an industry which would be capable of re-equipping and organizing not only the whole of our industry but also of our transport and our agriculture on a Socialist basis . . . create in the country all the necessary technical and economic prerequisites for increasing to the utmost the defensive capacity of the country, enable it to organize determined resistance to any and every attempt at military intervention or military aggression from outside.

In 1931 he emphasized the point:

No, comrades . . . the pace must not be slackened! On the contrary, we must quicken it as much as is within our powers and possibilities . . . . To slacken the pace would mean to lag behind and those who lag behind are beaten. We do not want to be beaten . . . . We are fifty or a hundred years behind the advanced countries. We must make good this lag in ten years. Either we do it or they will crush us.

WHICH INDUSTRIES?

During the 1890s Witte had relied upon foreign capital to finance Russian industrialization (p. 8). Stalin knew that there would be little if any foreign capital forthcoming to help the Bolshevik plan. Russia had to supply her own

resources and managed to increase the capital investment from 1.7 billion roubles in 1928 to 7 billion roubles in 1931, 'the heroic year', after which it fell off to an annual average of 5 billion roubles. Most of this investment was channelled into heavy industry (picture 43) and little investment was allowed in light industry which produced consumer goods. The result can be seen in the following table.

Commodity	Year			
(million tonnes)	1913	1928	1932	1940
Coal	29	35	64	166
Pig-iron	4	3	6	15
Steel	4	4	6	18
Oil	9	11	22	31
Electricity (billion kilowatts)	2	5	13	48

42   Harvesting in Russia, October 1923. Notice the old-fashioned equipment and the use of women workers — as had been the case in Britain in the early nineteenth century. Russia was a backward country.

THE COST OF INDUSTRIALIZATION

Over a third of the nation's budget was spent on industrialization, and there was little left for light, consumer goods industries, so that there were few goods in the shops and the Russians' standard of living fell below the low level it had reached under NEP rule.

RUSSIAN LABOUR

Russian folk-memories were dominated by the old days in which only the serf owner gained from a serf's hard work. Russians were used to staying away from work whenever they felt like it, to wrecking a machine so that they could have time off, and to slacking as soon as the supervisor had his back turned. Stalin tried to change all this, although he never succeeded in curing the Russians of heavy drinking and 'the morning-after' absenteeism. Teams of workers were made to compete against each other. When one reached a new, high level of output all teams were then forced to produce the same amount (picture 44). Grumblers and slackers were rounded up and sent to work in labour camps which built canals, railways in the Arctic and irrigation canals in the desert. Absenteeism was punished by the loss of the foodcard and even of housing.

57

44   Stakhanov explaining to fellow-workers his method of work. He was adopted as a symbol by the Stalinist government, which then used his outstanding production figures as examples for other workers to imitate.

STALIN AND THE PEASANT

The revolution had distributed land to 25 million families who were willing or able to supply only small amounts of food for sale. But if Russia was to finance her own industrialization there had to be a great increase in the amount exported as payment for the imports of machinery. And a larger industrial workforce needed more food.

The right-wing, led by Bukharin, had argued that industrialization would take place, but slowly 'at the pace of a tortoise' under NEP. The peasants, anxious to buy more of the goods produced by the NEP men, would produce more food to get the money they needed. So, extra grain would be available — for the workers and for export. But, argued the left-wing, this meant that industrialization could only take place if the peasants became better-off. A prosperous peasantry had been Stolypin's dream (p. 22).

58

Such a prosperous group would be the enemy of Communism. In 1929 after he had launched the first Five-Year Plan (p. 55) Stalin said:

.... Can we advance our socialized industry at an accelerated rate while having to rely on an agricultural base, such as is provided by small peasant farming, which is incapable of expanded reproduction, and which, in addition, is the predominant force in our national economy? No, we cannot. Can the Soviet government and the work of Socialist construction be, for any length of time, based on two different foundations: on the foundation of the most large-scale and concentrated Socialist industry and on the foundation of the most scattered and backward, small-commodity peasant farming? No, they cannot. Sooner or later this would be bound to end in the complete collapse of the whole national economy. What, then, is the solution? The solution lies in enlarging the agricultural units, in making agriculture capable of accumulation, of expanded reproduction, and in thus changing the agricultural base of our national economy. But how are the agricultural units to be enlarged? There are two ways of doing this. There is the capitalist way, which is to enlarge the agricultural units by introducing capitalism in agriculture — a way which leads to the impoverishment of the peasantry and to the development of capitalist enterprises in agriculture. We reject this way as incompatible with the Soviet economic system. There is a second way: the Socialist way, which is to set up collective farms and state farms, the way which leads to the amalgamation of the small peasant farms into large collective farms, technically and scientifically equipped, and to the squeezing out of the capitalist elements from agriculture. We are in favour of this second way.

COLLECTIVE FARMING

During the 1920s there had been various attempts to get the peasants to join some form of collective farm. In the *toz* the peasant kept his own land but joined with his neighbours to share machinery. In the *commune* people gave up private property altogether, lived in dormitories and had their children looked after in communal nurseries. Between these two extremes was the *kolkhoz* or collective farm on which the

peasants from two or three villages kept some private plot of land but handed the bulk of property over to the kolkhoz which was managed by an elected committee under a chairman appointed by the local Party. All the work was done by brigades of workers of between 50 and 100. Each kolkhoz had its annual production target — of grain, chickens and so on. The government took about 15 per cent of the output at a fixed low price; and another 5 per cent at a higher, near-market price. Another 15 per cent had to be paid to the Machine Tractor Station (picture 46) which supplied each collective with the machinery it needed; the collective's committee would then set aside part of the output for seed requirements, reserves in case of harvest failure in the next year and the remainder — about one-quarter of the whole — was distributed among the collective farmers on the basis of the number of workdays they had put in on the collective.

Each member of the kolkhoz owned his garden tools, garden, house and a limited number of animals — a cow, one or two pigs, chickens, rabbits and so on. There was a temptation for the people to concentrate their efforts on their own plots and to slack at their collective duties.

45 Mechanization on a collective in the Ukraine, 1936.

46   The farmers on a collective in the North Caucasian
Territory welcoming the arrival of a column of tractors
in 1930.

STALIN AND COLLECTIVIZATION

After 1927 Stalin encouraged peasants to join collectives. They were reluctant to do so, preferring their own small farms to the much larger, impersonal kolkhozes where they would lose most of their land. The peasants used their own methods of fighting the government. In 1929 they consumed most of what they produced because of the shortage of consumer goods resulting from the start of the Five-Year Plan (p. 55). The result was great hardship. There was bread rationing, food queues and grumbling in the towns. Stalin then announced 'a war on the peasants', for which he had previously condemned his opponents (p. 54). A million of the better-off peasants, or kulaks, had their property seized so that collectives could be formed. Once this policy was announced the peasants slaughtered their beasts and sold the meat. In many places peasants fought with the troops sent to help Party members involved in forcible collectivization. There were 300 peasant risings in 1930 alone. Resisters were deported to the icy north or the burning deserts. Serge, a witness to some of the suffering, wrote:

> Trainloads of deported peasants left for the icy north, the forests, the steppes, the deserts. These were the whole populations, denuded of everything; the old folk starved to death in mid-journey, new-born babies were buried on the banks of the roadside, and each wilderness had its crop of little crosses of boughs, or white wood. Other populations, dragging all their mean possessions on wagons, rushed towards the frontiers of Poland, Rumania, and China and crossed them — by no means intact, to be sure — in spite of the machine-guns . . . .

It is not known how many kulaks died as a result of this forcible collectivization; estimates vary from 13 million to 30 million. In addition there were at least three million deaths from malnutrition and disease during the Great Famine of 1932-33.

47 A painting entitled *Collective workers on holiday*. In Stalin's Russia, all art, poetry, literature and music had to glorify the worker and the Communist government.

STALIN DRAWS BACK

In 1930 Stalin called a halt in the campaign after two-thirds of all Russian farms had been organized into collectives but at a great cost. After the horrors of the famine the policy was resumed but at a slower pace and by 1939 collectivization was complete although the Russian peasant was still more concerned with working his own private plot than with work on the collective farm.

THE TERROR AND THE PURGES, 1934-39

The Cheka (p. 46), abolished by Lenin in 1922, had been replaced by the OGPU which became hated and feared during the collectivization programme when its agents arrested thousands of kulaks. In 1934 OGPU merged with the People's Commissariat for Internal Affairs which from its Russian initials is known as NKVD. It was this organization which was used by Stalin during the 'Terror'.

On 1 December 1934 Stalin's colleague, Kirov, the city boss of Leningrad (p. 54), was murdered. Yagoda, the head of the NKVD, organized the arrest and imprisonment of Zinoviev, Kamenev and other eminent Party members — who might have been considered possible opponents of Stalin's industrial and agricultural policies. During 1934 the number of Party members fell from 3.5 million to 2.7 million. The fall continued throughout 1935 at the end of which there were fewer than 2 million members of the Russian Communist Party.

In August 1936 Zinoviev, Kamenev and others (The Sixteen) were brought to public trial after almost two years of 'treatment' at the hands of the NKVD. They confessed to whatever charges were levelled at them — even when it was obvious that at least some of the charges were false. The best explanation for the confessions has been given by a former Communist, Arthur Koestler, who has written:

> Although several factors contributed to bringing the men to the point of making these confessions, they made them at the last in the sincere conviction that this was their sole remaining service to the Party and the Revolution. They sacrificed honour as well as life to

defend the hated regime of Stalin, because it contained the last faint gleam of hope for that better world to which they had consecrated themselves in early youth.

A Russian prisoner wrote:

They kept me five months in isolation; without papers, without anything to read, without mail, without contact with the outside world, without visits from my family, I was hungry, I suffered from solitude; they demanded of me that I confess having committed an act of sabotage that never took place; I refused to take upon myself crimes that had never been committed, but they told me that if I was really for the Soviet power, as I said I was, I ought to confess in this affair, for the Soviet power needed my confession; that I need have no fear of the consequences; the Soviet regime would take into consideration my open-hearted confession, and would give me the opportunity to work and to make good my mistakes through work. At the same time I would have visits from my family, letters, walks, newspapers. But if I persisted in maintaining silence I would be subjected to pitiless repression, and not myself alone, but my wife and children also. For months I resisted; but my situation become so intolerable that nothing, it seemed to me, could be worse; in any case I had become indifferent to everything the examining judge demanded of me.

The 16 accused were found guilty, and shot. Their trial was followed by the arrest of Stalin's allies in 1938, Rykov, Bukharin and Tomsky — and by the dismissal of Yagoda from the leadership of the NKVD, whose new head, Yezhov, organized the arrest, trial and imprisonment of many thousands. State prisons became overcrowded and many thousands of prisoners were then taken to the huge labour camps of which we now know a great deal because of the writings of former prisoners such as Solzhenitsyn.

In 1937 Radek was the leader of 'The Seventeen' put on trial. Later, Marshal Tukhachevsky — Commander-in-Chief of the Red Army and a hero of the Civil War — was executed along with seven other generals. In 1938 there was the 'Trial of the Twenty-One', when Rykov was joined by Bukharin and, ironically, Yagoda (p. 61). Having thus got rid of all opposition within the Party and in the army, Stalin turned on the NKVD. Thousands of agents were shot, Yezhov dismissed and replaced by Beria. By 1938 Stalin had eliminated almost all the delegates who had attended the 1934 Party Congress, almost all the leaders of the Revolution and almost all possible opponents. He had replaced them with his own, younger, supporters and could boast that Russia was united, industrially strong and more prepared to meet any possible attack from the West. But the cost had been great — in agriculture and industry and in the many concentration camps where about 14 million people were rotting to death.

YOUNG HISTORIAN

A

1 Read Lenin's *Testament* (p. 53) and explain the meaning of:
   (a) 'boundless authority', to show how it had been achieved and how it was used;
   (b) 'not sure ... caution', showing why Lenin should have thought this and how Stalin's later career proved Lenin to have been correct.

2 Use the index as an aid to write a brief career of Trotsky. Explain why many Bolsheviks (a) feared him; (b) opposed his policies towards (i) world revolution, (ii) a war on the peasants and (iii) a crash programme for industrialization.

3 Explain why NEP tended to benefit the peasants. Explain why this led to left-wing criticism of NEP and show that such criticism was bound to grow with Russian industrialization.

4 Read the extract from Stalin's speech (p. 55) and make a list of the various reasons why Stalin wanted rapid and massive

industrialization. Who had been demoted for proposing this policy?

5 Explain why Stalin believed that collectivization was essential if Russia were to be properly and quickly industrialized. Read Stalin's speech (p. 58) and show that there were political reasons for the adoption of the policy of collectivization.

6 Explain how a kolkhoz worked. Why were the kulaks opposed to collectivization?

B

1 Write a letter which might have been sent by one of Stalin's supporters who was local Party secretary somewhere in Russia between 1922 and 1924.

2 Write the letter which might have been sent by a kulak criticizing Trotsky's proposals for a war on the peasants.

3 Write the letters which might have been sent from Leningrad (a) in 1923 when Trotsky was advocating more industrialization and a war on the peasants; (b) in 1925 after Trotsky's defeat; (c) in 1925-26 complaining about the lack of food in the city.

4 Write the letter which might have been sent from Moscow by someone who saw Trotsky's attempt to overthrow Stalin in 1927.

5 Write the letters which might have been sent by someone from the right-wing complaining of the shortage of goods in the 1930s.

6 Write the letters which might have been sent by (a) someone from the right-wing explaining the 'pace of the tortoise' (p. 58) and (b) someone from the left-wing complaining of the food shortages in 1928 and the increasing prosperity of the kulaks.

7 Write the letters which might have been sent from a collective by (a) the Party official sent to take charge; (b) an Army officer sent to help him force the peasants into accepting collectivization; and (c) a kulak on why he was opposed to it and how he hoped to prevent it taking place.

8 Write the letter which might have been written by the wife of Zinoviev or Kamenev during their trial.

C

Write the headlines which might have appeared above reports on:

(a) Stalin's achievements, 1917-22 (You might make several, if you wish);

(b) Stalin's appointment as General Secretary;

(c) Trotsky's demand for a war on the peasants, 1923;

(d) Lenin's funeral;

(e) the publication of *Lessons of October*;

(f) the expulsion of Trotsky from office, *or* from the Politburo;

(g) the apologies by Zinoviev and Kamenev;

(h) the achievement of Stakhanov (pictures 43 and 44);

(i) Stalin's war on the kulaks;

(j) the trials of (a) Zinoviev and Kamenev; (b) Rykov; (c) Tukhachevsky; (d) Yagoda.

D

1 Make a graph to illustrate the tables on p. 56.

2 Make a chart to show (a) how Stalin first used Zinoviev and Kamenev against Trotsky; (b) how they adopted Trotsky's policies and were overthrown by Stalin; and (c) how Stalin himself then adopted these same policies after 1928.

SOVIET RUSSIA AND THE WEST, 1918-1945

THE WORLD REVOLUTION?

On 26 October 1917 the Lenin government issued a Decree on Peace which abolished secret diplomacy, condemned annexation of other countries' territory, declared an armistice and called on workers in Britain, France and Germany to support the movement for peace. Trotsky, the Commissar for Foreign Affairs, described this as 'active internationalism' and boasted, 'I will issue a few revolutionary proclamations to the peoples of the world and then shut up shop.' The Bolsheviks believed that world revolution would take place once the workers of the industrial world had seen how successful the Russians had been.

In 1918 and 1919 there were local attempts at Communist revolutions in Hungary and Germany. In each case they were easily, if bloodily, suppressed. In 1919 Russia invaded Poland to help get the world revolution started. Polish nationalists, led by Pilsudski, resisted, invading the Ukraine in April 1920. The Reds counter-attacked but at the battle of the Vistula (August 1920) were heavily defeated. The Red Army was not going to be able to spark off a world revolution. Bolshevik foreign policy had to be re-thought, just as did its economic policy (pp 55-61).

THE COMINTERN AND LITVINOV

An international organization, the Comintern, was set up to supervise the work of Communist parties throughout the world. Many western politicians suspected the Comintern and its master, Russia, of trying to create revolutions.

After Trotsky's dismissal (p. 54) a new Commissar for Foreign Affairs, Litvinov, was promoted. He signed a number of defensive treaties with the smaller countries of Eastern Europe. He also helped to improve trade relations between Russia and the capitalist West, the only possible source of the machine-tools and other goods needed for Russian industrialization (pp 54-59). To pay for these imports, Russia sent her grain, and the need to increase grain exports helps explain the policy of collectivization (p. 59).

THE TREATY OF RAPALLO, 1922

Germany had been harshly treated by the Treaty of Versailles (see the companion volume *Europe in the Twentieth Century*). The anti-German Allies had once tried to overthrow the Bolshevik government (pp. 46-48) and still retained a fear of the possibilities of the world revolution (picture 48). Both Germany and Russia were treated as 'outsiders' by Britain, France and the USA. In 1922 Russia signed the Treaty of Rapallo with its former enemy, Germany, which became the first country to give formal recognition to the Bolshevik government. German industrialists were invited to help in the development of the Russian iron, steel and coal industries. In return the Russians allowed the Germans to use Russian bases and

48 The *Daily Mail* for 25 October 1924, with its alleged Zinoviev letter.

64

CIVIL WAR PLOT BY SOCIALISTS' MASTERS.

OSCOW ORDERS TO OUR REDS.

REAT PLOT DISCLOSED YESTERDAY.

PARALYSE THE ARMY AND NAVY."

ND MR. MACDONALD WOULD LEND RUSSIA OUR MONEY!

DOCUMENT ISSUED BY FOREIGN OFFICE

AFTER "DAILY MAIL" HAD SPREAD THE NEWS.

A "very secret" letter of instruction from Moscow, which ublish below, discloses a great Bolshevik plot to paralyse British Army and Navy and to plunge the country into war.

The letter is addressed by the Bolsheviks of Moscow to Soviet Government's servants in Great Britain, the Com st Party, who in turn are the masters of Mr. Ramsay Donald's Government, which has signed a treaty with ow whereby the Soviet is to be guaranteed a "loan" of ons of British money.

The letter is signed by Zinoviev, the Dictator of Petrograd, ident of the Third (Moscow) International, and is addressed A. McManus, the British representative on the executive of International, who returned from Moscow to London on ber 18 to take part in the general election campaign.

Our information is that official copies of the letter, which ed September 15, were delivered to the Foreign Secretary, Ramsay MacDonald, and the Home Secretary, Mr. Arthur rson, immediately after it was received some weeks ago. On esday afternoon copies were officially circulated by the Executive rities to high officers of the Army and Navy.

copy of the document came into the possession of *The Daily Mail*, we felt it our duty to make it public. We circulated printed to other London morning newspapers yesterday afternoon. on the Foreign Office decided to issue it, together with a protest, yesterday, which the British Government has sent to M. Rakov- the Bolshevik Chargé d'Affaires in London.

The salient passages of Moscow's plot letter are:

Armed warfare must be preceded by a struggle against the inations to compromise which are embedded among the ority of British workmen, against the ideas of evolution and eful extermination of capitalism.

Only then will it be possible to count on complete success n armed insurrection.

From your last report it is evident that agitation-propaganda k in the Army is weak and the Navy a very little better. . . . It ld be desirable to have [propaganda-agitation] cells in all the s of the troops, among factories working on munitions and at itary store depots.

The military section of the British Communist Party further fers from a lack of specialists, the future directors of the tish Red Army . . . . . It is time you thought of forming h a group.

The British protest is signed, in the absence of the Foreign Sec- Mr. MacDonald, by Mr. J. D. Gregory, Permanent Assistant retary of the Foreign Office. It requests a reply "without delay."

The text of this protest is in another column.

THE BRITISH RED ARMY.

R COMMUNISTS TOLD TO FIND GENERAL STAFF.

The text of the civil war document is:

VERY SECRET.

EXECUTIVE COMMITTEE
THIRD
MMUNIST INTERNATIONAL
PRESIDIUM
Sept. 15th 1924.
MOSCOW

TO THE CENTRAL COMMITTEE
BRITISH COMMUNIST PARTY.

ear Comrades,

The time is approaching for the Parliament of England to consider e Treaty concluded between the Governments of Great Britain and e S.S.S.R. for the purpose of ratification. The fierce campaign raised y the British bourgeoisie around the question shows that the majority f the same, together with reactionary circles, are against* the reaty for the purpose of breaking off an agreement consolidating the ties between the proletariats of the two countries leading to the restora- ion of normal relations between England and the S.S.S.R.

The proletariat of Great Britain, which pronounced its weighty word when danger threatened of a break-off of the past negotiations, and compelled the Government of MacDonald to conclude the Treaty, must show the greatest possible energy in the further struggle for ratification and against the endeavours of British capitalists to compel Parliament to annul it.

It is indispensable to stir up the masses of the British proletariat, to bring into movement the army of unemployed proletarians, whose position can be improved only after a loan has been granted to the S.S.S.R. for the restoration of her economics and when business collaboration between the British and Russian proletariats has been put in order. It is imperative that the group in the Labour Party sympathising with the Treaty should bring increased pressure to bear upon the Government and parliamentary circles in favour of the ratification of the Treaty.

Keep close observation over the leaders of the Labour Party, because these may easily be found in the leading strings of the bourgeoisie. The foreign policy of the Labour Party as it is already represents an inferior copy of the policy of the Curzon Government. Organise a campaign of disclosure of the foreign policy of MacDonald.

ARMED INSURRECTION.

The IKKI [Executive Committee, third (Communist) International] will willingly place at your disposal the wide material in its possession regarding the activities of British imperialism in the Middle and Far East. In the meanwhile, however, strain every nerve in the struggle for the ratification of the Treaty, in favour of a continuation of negotiations regarding the regulation of relations between the S.S.S.R. and England. A settlement of relations between the two countries will assist in the revolutionising of the international and British proletariat not less than a successful rising in any of the working districts of England, as the establishment of close contact between the British and Russian proletariat, the exchange of delegations and workers, etc., will make it possible for us to extend and develop the propaganda of ideas of Leninism in England and the Colonies. Armed warfare must be preceded by a struggle against the inclinations to compromise which are embedded among the majority of British workmen, against the ideas of evolution and peaceful extermination of capitalism. Only then will it be possible to count upon complete success of an armed

Zinoviev, whose real name is Apfelbaum.

insurrection. In Ireland and the Colonies the case is different; there there is a national question, and this represents too great a factor for success for us to waste time on a prolonged preparation of the working class.

But even in England, as in other countries where the workers are politically developed, events themselves may more rapidly revolutionise the working masses than propaganda. For instance, a strike movement, repressions by the Government, etc.

From your last report it is evident that agitation-propaganda work in the Army is weak, in the Navy a very little better. Your explanation that the quality of the members attracted justifies the quantity is right in principle, nevertheless it would be desirable to have cells in all the units of the troops, particularly among those quartered in the large centres of the country, and also among factories working on munitions and at military store depots. We request that the most particular attention be paid to these latter.

A CLASS WAR.

In the event of danger of war, with the aid of the latter and in contact with the transport workers, it is possible to paralyse all the military preparations of the bourgeoisie, and make a start in turning an imperialist war into a class war. Now more than ever we should be on our guard. Attempts at intervention in China show that world imperialism is still full of vigour and is once more making endeavours to restore its shaken position and cause a new war, which as its final objective is to bring about the break-up of the Russian proletariat and the suppression of the budding world revolution, and further would lead to the enslavement of the colonial peoples. "Danger of War," "The Bourgeoisie seeks War; Capital fresh Markets"—these are the slogans which you must familiarise the masses with, with which you must go to work into the mass of the proletariat. These slogans will open to you the doors of comprehension of the masses, will help you to capture them and march under the banner of Communism.

The Military Section of the British Communist Party, so far as we are aware, further suffers from a lack of specialists, the future directors of the British Red Army.

It is time you thought of forming such a group, which, together with the leaders, might be, in the event of an outbreak of active strife, the brain of the military organisation of the party.

Go attentively through the lists of the military "cells," detailing from them the more energetic and capable men, turn attention to the more talented military specialists who have for one reason or another left the Service and hold Socialist views. Attract them into the ranks of the Communist Party if they desire honestly to serve the proletariat and desire in the future to direct not the blind mechanical forces in the service of the bourgeoisie but a national army.

Form a directing operative head of the Military Section.

Do not put this off to a future moment, which may be pregnant with events and catch you unprepared.

Desiring you all success, both in organisation and in your struggle,

With Communist Greetings,
President of the Presidium
of the IKKI,
ZINOVIEV.
Member of the Presidium,
McManus.
Secretary, KUUSINEN.

FOREIGN OFFICE PROTEST.

REPLY WITHOUT DELAY REQUESTED.

The following is the text of the letter sent yesterday by Mr. J. D. Gregory to M. Rakovski, the Chargé d'Affaires in London of the Soviet Union:—

FOREIGN OFFICE,
October 24, 1924.

SIR,—I have the honour to invite your attention to the enclosed copy of a letter which has been received by the Central Committee of the British Communist Party from the Presidium of the Executive Committee of the Communist International, over the signature of Monsieur Zinoviev, its president, dated September 15.

The letter contains instructions to British subjects to work for the violent overthrow of existing institutions in this country, and for the subversion of his Majesty's armed forces as a means to that end.

2. It is my duty to inform you that his Majesty's Government cannot allow this propaganda and must regard it as a direct interference from outside in British domestic affairs.

3. No one who understands the constitution and the relationships of the Communist International will doubt its intimate connection and contact with the Soviet Government. No Government will ever tolerate an arrangement with a foreign Government by which the latter is in formal diplomatic relations of a correct kind with it, while at the same time a propagandist body organically connected with that foreign Government encourages and even orders subjects of the former to plot and plan revolutions for its overthrow.

Such conduct is not only a grave departure from the rules of international comity, but a violation of specific and solemn undertakings repeatedly given to his Majesty's Government.

4. So recently as June 4 of last year the Soviet Government made the following solemn agreement with his Majesty's Government:—

The Soviet Government undertakes not to support with funds or in any other form persons or bodies or agencies

McManus

or institutions whose aim is to spread discontent or to foment rebellion in any part of the British Empire . . . and to impress upon its officers and officials the full and continuous observance of these conditions.

5. Moreover, in the Treaty which his Majesty's Government recently concluded with your Government, still further provision was made for the faithful execution of an analogous undertaking which is essential to the existence of good and friendly relations between the two countries.

His Majesty's Government mean that these undertakings shall be carried out both in the letter and in the spirit, and it cannot accept the contention that while the Soviet Government undertakes obligations, a political body, as powerful as itself, is to be allowed to conduct a propaganda and support it with money,

Continued in Next Column.

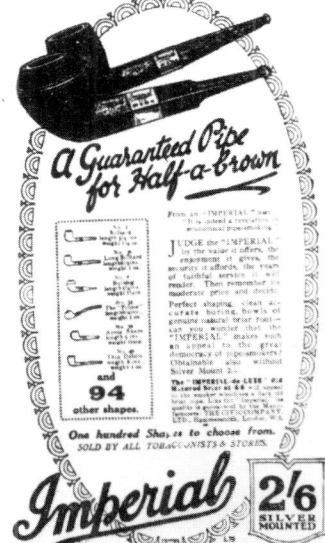

LATEST NEWS

SPEAKER'S DEATH AT MEETING.

When concluding a speech in support of Mr. Frank Hobson, Conservative candidate in the Platting division of Manchester, at St. Stephen's School, Conran-street, Manchester, last night, ex-Councillor Thomas McRoy, of Blakley, collapsed and died.

He had just pronounced the words "for God, for King, and for country" when he fell back in his chair.

Four members of the audience fainted.

£5,000 OR £5 A WEEK FOR LIFE.

"DAILY MAIL" ELECTION COMPETITION.

POST FORMS NOW.

To-day the entry-form for the *Daily Mail's* great Election Competition is at the top of Column 4, Page 2.

To-morrow it will be printed in every copy of *The Weekly Dispatch*, and it will also appear in *The Daily Mail* on Monday and Tuesday next.

These will represent the final chances of winning the great prize of

FIVE THOUSAND POUNDS
OR
£5 A WEEK FOR LIFE.

Forms which have already been completed should be sent *at once* to the address given below.

There is no entry fee, and the prize must be won.

Cut out the form carefully, setting against the name of each party the number of candidates you estimate will be elected holding those political views.

Forecasts must be sent to—

"ELECTION COMPETITION,
THE DAILY MAIL,
7, PILGRIM-STREET,
LONDON, E.C. 4."

Each forecast must be on a separate entry form, cut from *The Daily Mail* or from *The Weekly Dispatch*. Forms which arrive after the first post on October 29 will be disqualified.

In the event of a tie or ties the sum of £5,000 will be divided among the successful competitors.

There are 615 seats in the House of Commons, so your estimate should add up to this total.

In the last Parliament there were, at the dissolution:

CONSERVATIVES	257
LABOUR AND COMMUNISTS	193
LIBERALS	158
INDEPENDENT	6

One Conservative seat was unfilled pending a by-election.

THE ENTRY FORM AND RULES ARE AT THE TOP OF COLUMN 4, PAGE 2.

21 DEATHS MYSTERY.

14 WOMEN VICTIMS IN A MOTOR SHIP WRECK.

FROM OUR OWN CORRESPONDENT.

Riga, Friday.

Riga is mystified by the wreck of a motor-assisted sailing vessel, the Beindeer, which ran ashore in Riga bay in yesterday's storm. Twenty-one people lost their lives, including 14 women.

Twelve bodies have been washed ashore, and 9 people were found dead in the hold of the vessel, apparently suffocated by petrol fumes.

Among the dead are the crew of three.

The authorities are investigating the matter and believe that the drinking of vodka, the alcoholic drink commonly consumed in Russia, is the cause.

Continued from Preceding Column.

which is in direct violation of the official agreement.

The Soviet Government either has or has not the power to make such agreements. If it has the power it is its duty to carry them out and see that the other parties are not deceived. If it has not this power and if responsibilities which belong to the State in other countries are in Russia in the keeping of private and irresponsible bodies the Soviet Government ought not to make agreements which it knows it cannot carry out.

6. I should be obliged if you would be good enough to let me have the observations of your Government on this subject without delay.

I have the honour to be,
with high consideration, Sir,
Your obedient Servant
(In the absence of the Secretary of State)
(Sd.) J. D. GREGORY.

M. C. Rakovski
Etc., etc., etc.

THE MASTER ASSASSIN.

ZINOVIEV WHO SIGNED DEATH WARRANTS OF THOUSANDS.

Under the Czars, Zinoviev, who is 41, was associated with the Terrorist group who were responsible for all political assassinations in Russia. In 1906 he was arrested for being concerned in publishing a paper which incited its readers to a bloody revolution and the entire destruction of the bourgeoisie.

Between 1915 and 1917 he denounced the Allies on every possible occasion, and by means of smuggled correspondence got into touch with British pacifists. Getting back to Russia in March 1917 he helped to demoralise the Russian army, and on the success of the Bolshevist coup d'état became the leader of the Petrograd Soviet and the master assassin.

As the head of the Petrograd Commune he signed the death warrants of thousands of men, women, and youths. He organised the Secret Police of Petrograd.

AGITATIONS OF McMANUS.

Arthur McManus started life as a fitter at Liverpool. For his activities on the Clyde during the war, as editor of the Glasgow Socialist, he was deported to Edinburgh.

At one time he was in touch with the Industrial Workers of the World, an organisation concerned in dynamite outrages in the United States and Australia.

After a visit to Russia last year he said there was a sense of security there that existed in no other country.

He is chairman of the British Communist Party.

THE PREMIER'S TRUST.

Hours after the Foreign Office yesterday had sent the note to the Bolsheviks stating that their "Very Secret" instruction is "a violation of specific and solemn undertakings repeatedly given to his Majesty's Government," Mr. Ramsay MacDonald, Secretary of State for Foreign Affairs, said at Taibach, in his Aberavon constituency:

I have no doubt that Russia will carry out the Treaties we have with her.

DE VALERA ARRESTED.

ULSTER POLICE ACTION.

Mr. de Valera, the Irish Republican leader, was arrested by the Ulster authorities last night when he entered the town hall at Newry, County Down, to address a meeting in support of the Republicans.

He was first served with an expulsion order by armed police. He refused to obey it and was bundled unceremoniously out of the hall. Miss Mary MacSwiney, one of his followers, tried to greet him, but the police intervened. Revolvers were drawn when the crowd showed signs of surging towards the constables.

De Valera's disguise consisted of leaving off his large, horn-rimmed spectacles. The Ulster police knew him only by his newspaper portraits, in which the spectacles figure prominently.

Newry had been agog with excitement at the prospect of Mr. de Valera attempting to evade the authorities and address the meeting.

The chief Republican election agent (at Dublin) has sent a telegram to the British Prime Minister and the Home Secretary relating to the arrest of de Valera and declaring: "This outrage was impossible without the connivance of the British Government, which decreed the elections, and which is responsible for proper conduct of them."

YOUR VOTE.

HOW AND WHERE TO RECORD IT.

It is the patriotic duty of every qualified man and woman to vote next Wednesday.

If you have any doubt about YOUR eligibility you should go to-day to the nearest principal post office and ask to see the local register of parliamentary electors. If your name is in this list you are entitled to vote. Your name will appear in the register of the district in which you resided on June 1 last.

WHERE TO VOTE.

Full information about the time and the place, the polling-booth, to vote will be given to you at the nearest Conservative or Liberal committee room.

The ballot is *absolutely secret*. A ballot paper is handed to the voter at the polling booth. On this paper you must write a cross (X) in the space provided on the right-hand side of the name of the candidate for whom you wish to vote. Nothing else must be written on the paper. It is important to note that the names of candidates are always arranged in alphabetical order.

HANGED IN PAIRS.

FOUR BANK BANDITS.

FROM OUR OWN CORRESPONDENT.

MONTREAL, Friday.

On two scaffolds dimly lighted by small lanterns four bandits were executed just before dawn this morning for the murder of a bank chauffeur in the "hold-up" of a Bank of Hochelaga collection car in April.

The men were Louis Morel, a former Montreal detective; Toney Frank, known as the King of the Underworld, Frank Gambino, and Giuseppe Serafini, who had just returned from his honeymoon in Italy.

Morel, once a famous athlete, stood like a Greek statue on the scaffold. Gambino fainted, but rallied. Frank faced death bravely; and Serafini kissed the priest and the gaol governor passionate adieus. The prison was heavily guarded by constables with fixed bayonets, and motor-cycle detachments patrolled all the roads.

PEKING CHANGES HANDS.

COUP WHILE CITY SLEPT.

GATES OPENED BY PLOTTERS.

CHRISTIAN GENERAL'S 'IRONSIDES.'

FROM OUR OWN CORRESPONDENT.

PEKING, Friday.

Yesterday's occupation of the capital by Feng Yu-hsiang, the "Christian general," who deserted and returned suddenly from the front with his "Ironsides," followed the entire collapse of the Peking Government forces in their fight against Chang Tso-lin, the War Lord of Manchuria.

Wu Pei-fu, the Commander-in-Chief of the Government forces, is reported to have fled aboard an Italian gunboat at Chinwangtao. Everything was arranged according to the plans of Chang Tso-lin.

The city is quiet and no trouble is anticipated.

FROM OUR OWN CORRESPONDENT.

MUKDEN, Friday.

Chang's Manchurian forces have now cut off 25,000 retreating Central Government troops between Shanhaikwan (near the Great Wall, about 200 miles east of Peking) and Chingwangtao. President Tsao Kun is a refugee in the Dutch Legation at Peking. General Wu must now surrender or fly to Japan.

FROM OUR OWN CORRESPONDENT.

HONG KONG, Friday.

The naval authorities here learn that Feng has issued a proclamation saying he intends to put an end to the war. It may also be his intention to replace the President, Tsao Kun, by Tuan Chi-jui, the former Premier.

The presidential palace is surrounded by troops. The only means of communication with Peking is by wireless.

THE PLOT.

PEKING, Friday.

A group of generals having decided to bring hostilities to an end secretly arranged for Feng's soldiers to take charge here while others took measures to prevent Wu Pei-fu's return. Early yesterday morning, while the city still slept, the Peking garrison troops opened the gates to Feng's men.

Bell Tower, Peking.

While most of the members of the Cabinet were not consulted in the plot, a group of prominent young Chinese, including Huang Fu, Minister of Education, and Dr. C. T. Wang, former Foreign Minister, took part inside Peking. This group asserts it is determined to bring hostilities to an end, after which it intends to call a round table conference.

The remainder of the war and other troops having reached Peking, General Feng has a total command of more than 40,000 men. Not a single shot was fired either during or after the coup d'état.

President Tsao Kun has issued a mandate ordering an immediate cessation of hostilities. Wu Pei-fu is dismissed from his present post and appointed "Chief Commissioner for the development of Kokonor" (a frontier lake just beyond the boundary of Kansu province). Both armies (the Peking forces and those of Chang Tso-lin) are ordered to maintain the status quo.—Reuter.

factories to re-equip and train that army which the Germans were forbidden to have by the Treaty of Versailles.

The other Western powers were horrified at the news of Rapallo. They quickly brought Germany back into the Western fold by signing the Treaty of Locarno (1925) in which Britain guaranteed the frontiers between France and Germany, France promised to defend Poland and Czechoslovakia against German aggression and Germany was invited to join the League of Nations. Russia was not invited to sign this Treaty. Nor was she invited to join the League, while Britain's refusal to guarantee Germany's eastern frontier seemed to be an invitation to Germany to expand eastward. This increased Russia's fear of the West, gave added strength to Stalin's arguments for 'socialism in one country' as opposed to Trotsky's call for a world revolution (p. 64) and was a major reason for the policy of industrialization adopted in 1928 (pp. 55-57).

RUSSIA AND THE FAR EAST

In the companion volume *China in the Twentieth Century*, it is explained why the leaders of the new, weak government of Nationalist China had sent a telegram of congratulations to Lenin and how Lenin's government helped that Chinese government led by Sun Yat-sen. Communist agents were sent to China to help organize the government, industry and agriculture. Chinese Officers went to Russia for their training and Russian officers returned with the first group to set up a military Academy near Canton.

The Russians hoped to use Sun Yat-sen's government and his Kuomingtang party (KMT) as a means of winning Communist control of China. Sun and the KMT hoped to use Russian aid to strengthen their own hold on China. Sun Yat-sen died in 1925, one year after Lenin. The new leader of China was Chiang Kai-shek who had been trained in Russia but who distrusted the Communists. In 1927 Chiang, aided by the Russians, drove northwards from Canton to attack the many war-lords ruling in the Chinese provinces. He was very successful but in the middle of his success he turned on the Chinese Communists, massacred over 5 000 in Shanghai in 1927 and forced the rest to go into hiding. Preparations for the attack were well-known.

Indeed, Serge, who was in Russia at the time writes:

.... We followed the preparation of the military coup whose only possible outcome was the massacre of the Shanghai proletariat. Zinoviev, Trotsky and Radek demanded an immediate change of line from the Central Committee ... to send the Shanghai Committee a telegram 'Defend yourselves if you have to!' and the Chinese Revolution would not have been beheaded .... But the Politbureau insisted on the subordination of the Communist Party to the Kuomingtang ....

On the very day before the Shanghai incident, Stalin came to the Bolshoi Theatre to explain his policy to the assembled activists of Moscow. The whole Party noted one of his winged remarks: 'We are told that Chiang Kaishek is making ready to turn against us again. I know that he is playing a cunning game with us, but it is he that will be crushed. We shall squeeze him like a lemon and then be rid of him.'

This speech was in the press at *Pravda* when we heard the terrible news. Troops were wiping out the working-class quarters of Shanghai with sabre and machine-gun.

There had always been Chinese Communists who had tried to base the revolutionary movement on the peasants. In the past they had been condemned by those who supported the policy of cooperating with the KMT and using the industrial workers as the basis for the revolution. After 1927 Mao Tse-tung, Chou En-lai and others won increasing support for their ideas of a peasant-based Chinese revolution. Inside Russia those who criticized Stalin for having let slip a chance to stop the Shanghai Massacres were arrested — a foretaste of the many later arrests (pp 61-62).

COMING TO TERMS WITH THE WEST

In 1933 Roosevelt gave USA recognition to China, and in 1934 Russia joined the League of Nations. In 1935 Stalin signed Treaties of Mutual Assistance with France and Czechoslovakia. Stalin was aware of Hitler's ambitions for 'living-space' in the east. Hitler had written:

This colossal Empire in the East is ripe for dissolution .... The future goal of our foreign policy ought to have in view the acquisition of such Eastern territory as is necessary for our German people.

Stalin feared that Russia would be unable to resist a German attack. This helps to explain the limited aid which Russia gave to the Republican Government of Spain when it was attacked by the Fascists under Franco (who received massive aid from Germany and Italy). Stalin was afraid that if he sent in an equal volume of aid to the Republican government, Germany might use this as an excuse to launch an all-out war on Russia.

In the companion volume *Europe in the Twentieth Century* it is shown how the road to World War 2 was paved with the policy of appeasement as Britain and France failed to act in the face of aggression by the dictators. In 1935 Mussolini invaded Abyssinia; in 1936 Hitler marched into the demilitarized zone along the Rhine; in 1938 Hitler's army marched into Austria. In no case did the British or French take any positive steps to halt the lawbreakers. Even worse, in 1938 Czechoslovakia was broken up by an agreement between the governments of Germany and Italy on the one hand and of Britain and France on the other. Stalin was entitled to believe that the democracies would not stand up to the dictators but might very well support a German move against Communist Russia, because of Western fears of a Russian-inspired world revolution (p. 64).

THE NAZI-SOVIET PACT, 1939

Early in 1939 Stalin decided to adopt a new policy towards Germany. Serge, the exiled revolutionary, writes:

It was during that same month of March that I read the *Pravda* report of Stalin's speech to the Eighteenth Party Congress. The Leader accused Britain and France of trying to 'sow discord between the Soviet Union and Germany'. A speech by Voroshilov confirmed the authenticity of the details of Soviet military power which had been published in a Nazi military review. Through Reiss and Krivitsky we were aware that Soviet agents had been in continual contact with the Nazi rulers. On 5

May, Litvinov, the advocate of 'collective security' and of the Politbureau's 'peace policy' within the League of Nations, resigned abruptly. These clues, among others, were a clear indication that Soviet policy would soon switch to collaboration with the Third Reich ....

On 23 August 1939 the rest of the world was astonished by the announcement of the Non-Aggression Pact between Russia and Germany. Hitler took advantage of this Pact to invade Poland (1 September 1939), which brought France and England, at last, to war (3 September). German troops smashed through weak and inadequate Polish defences. On 17 September Russian troops invaded Poland from the east and a new period of Russian imperialism had begun. During the winter of 1939-40 Russia occupied Estonia, Latvia and Lithuania and undertook what proved to be a costly and almost disastrous war against Finland which ended when the Finns signed the Treaty of Moscow (12 March 1940) which gave the Russians the territory they needed on which to build military bases. Russia also took the province of Bessarabia from Romania so that by the end of 1940 the Russian boundary on Europe had been pushed westwards along the line from Finland to the Black Sea.

BARBAROSSA, 22 JUNE 1941

By mid-1941 Hitler had conquered France and had realized that he was not going to be able to invade Britain. He then switched his attention back to the east. News of the plan for the invasion of Russia, code named *Barbarossa*, was leaked to the Russians by a secret agent working in Japan who gave the date for the start of the invasion. On 3 April Churchill, the British Prime Minister, also sent a message to warn Stalin of German preparations for the invasion. In spite of this, the Russians appear to have been caught by surprise by the invasion on 22 June 1941. Hundreds of Soviet aircraft were destroyed on their runways by German Luftwaffe attacks; the well-organized and experienced panzer divisions rolled over the endless plains (p. 3), capturing thousands of soldiers and forcing civilians to flee from their towns and villages.

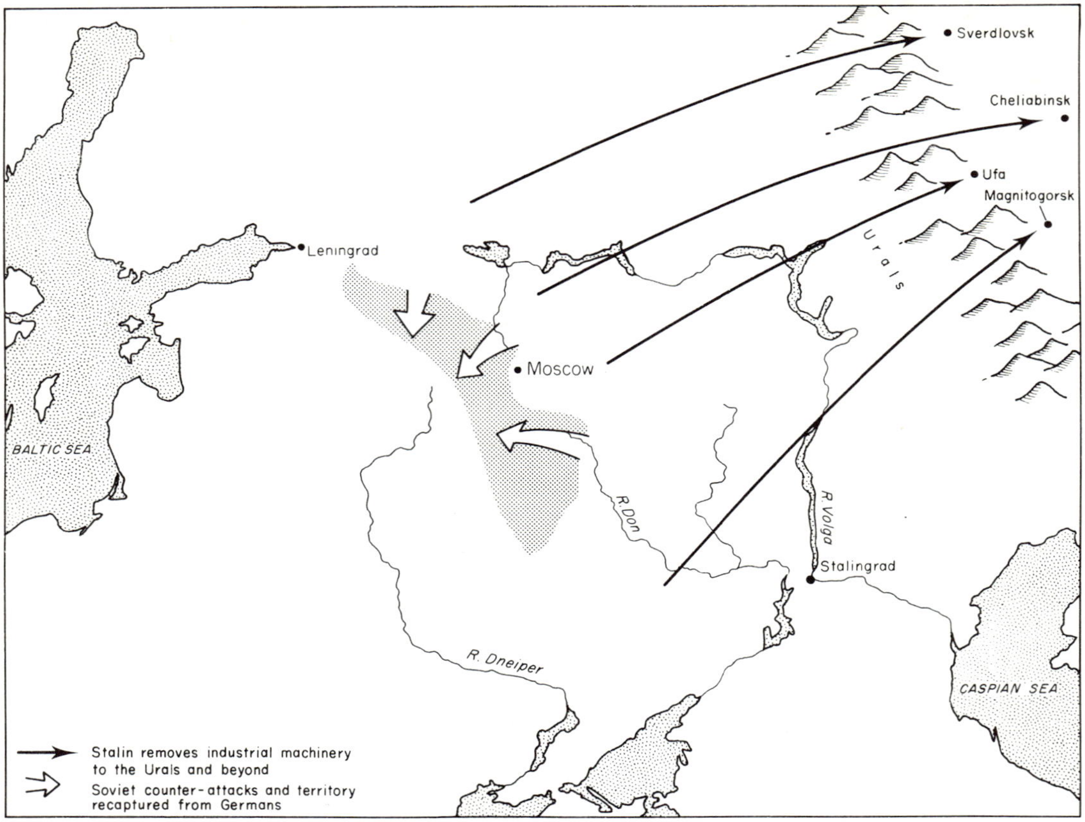

Sverdlovsk

Cheliabinsk

Ufa
Magnitogorsk

U r a l s

Leningrad

BALTIC SEA

Moscow

R Don

R Volga

Stalingrad

R Dneiper

CASPIAN SEA

Stalin removes industrial machinery
to the Urals and beyond

Soviet counter-attacks and territory
recaptured from Germans

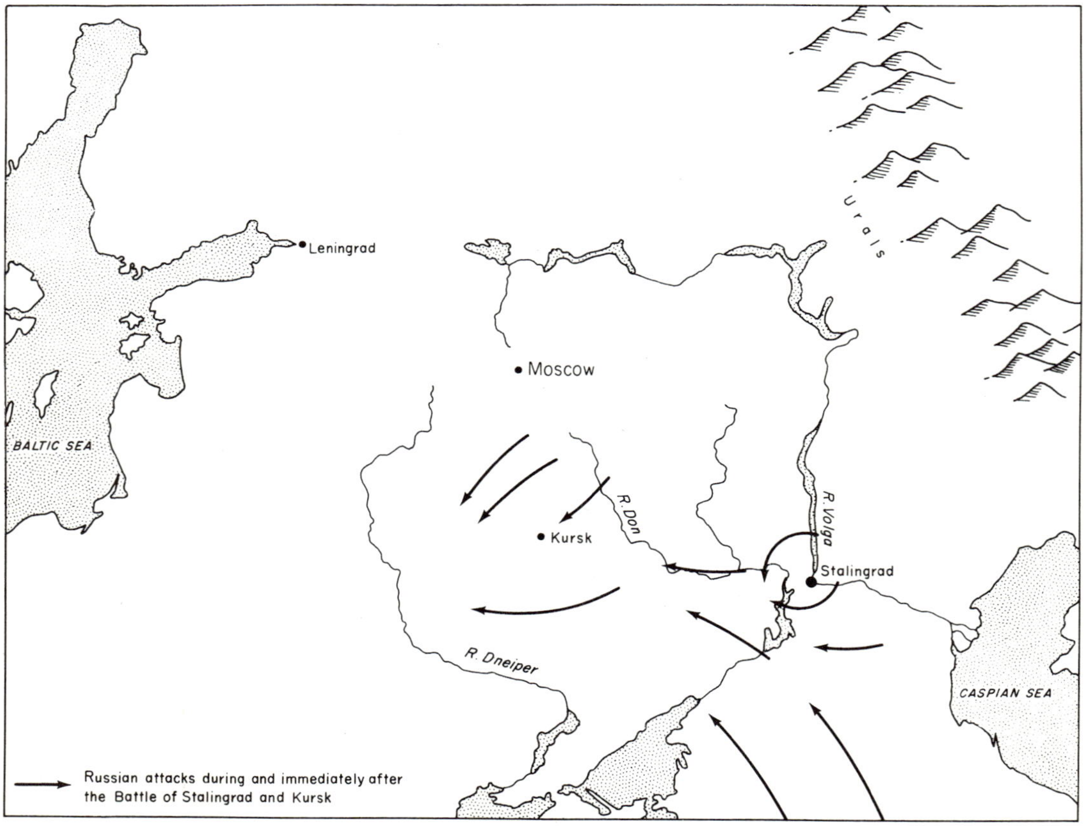

BALTIC SEA

Leningrad

U r a l s

Moscow

R Don

R Volga

Kursk

Stalingrad

R Dneiper

CASPIAN SEA

Russian attacks during and immediately after
the Battle of Stalingrad and Kursk

The German attack took place on a number of fronts. The Northern Army drove the Russians from their recently acquired Baltic provinces back to Leningrad, the old capital. A Central Army advanced on Moscow, the capital, where Stalin took control of Military Headquarters. A Southern Army advanced into the Ukraine, where the people of the Don area seemed to welcome the invaders, hoping for that independence for which Makhno had fought (p. 47). It was here that the first great battles were fought; at Uman and Kiev the Germans killed or captured 660 000 Russians, or one-third of the Russian army.

STALIN'S APPEAL TO THE PEOPLE

Stalin, the leader of the new Russia, then called on the people to use tactics which had been employed by Tsar Alexander I against Napoleon. In a broadcast to the people he demanded 'a scorched earth policy':

In case of a forced retreat . . . all rolling stock must be evacuated, the enemy must not be left a single engine, a single railway car, a single pound of grain or gallon of fuel. The collective farmers must drive all their cattle and turn over all their grain to the safe keeping of the authorities for transportation to the rear . . . . In areas occupied by the enemy, guerrillas, mounted and on foot, must be formed; sabotage groups must be organized to combat the enemy . . . blow up bridges and roads, damage telephone and telegraph lines, set fire to forests, stores and transport . . . .

The leader of the party which was supposed to advocate internationalism also used the 'patriotic card' in his appeal to the people (picture 50):

. . . . The enemy is cruel and implacable. He is about to seize our lands watered by the sweat of our brows, to seize our grain and oil secured by the labour of our hands. He is about to restore the rule of the landlords, to restore tsarism, to destroy the national culture and

50   Partisan fighters in the Smolensk area, 1943.

ВСЕ ДЛЯ ПОБЕДЫ!

ФРОНТУ ОТ ЖЕНЩИН СССР

51 A poster calling on women workers to produce more munitions for the war against Nazi Germany.

the national existence as states of the Russians . . . there must be no room in our ranks for whimperers and cowards, for panic-mongers and deserters; our people must know no fear in the fight and must selflessly join our patriotic war of liberation against the fascist enslavers . . . .

'GENERAL WINTER', 1941

During the summer and autumn German troops advanced along a long front. By September 1941 Leningrad was encircled, its people manning barricades to resist German advance. A girl wrote:

A cold terrible winter was approaching. Together with their bombs, enemy planes were dropping down leaflets. They said that they would raze Leningrad to the ground. They said we would all die of hunger. They thought they would frighten us, but they filled us with

70

renewed strength . . . . Leningrad did not let the enemy into its gates. The city was starving but it lived and worked, and kept sending to the front more and more new detachments of its sons and daughters.

In 1813 Napoleon had described the harsh Russian winter as the most effective obstacle to his plan for the conquest of Russia. In 1941 and 1942 the weather, nicknamed 'General Winter', came to the aid of the Russians once again.

The Germans had advanced towards Moscow which was under siege. The German commander, Guderian, wanted to make an all-out attack on the Russian capital. Hitler insisted on switching the main attack to the south and so Moscow was saved. The Battle of Moscow which took place in October-December 1941 was won by the Russians commanded by one of the new younger officers, Zhukov, who was helped by Hitler's decision to attack in the south and by the effects of the harsh Russian winter on the Germans who had inadequate clothing and whose tanks and lorries were not supplied with anti-freeze. By December 1941 Moscow was saved; the Germans had suffered their first defeat in the eastern war. Counter-attack early in 1942 drove the Germans back although it was not clear for how long.

SPRING OFFENSIVE, 1942

The Germans had suffered badly during the long winter. In a Russian report of an interview with a German prisoner we read:

'We are retreating because of the cold. We thought the Russian campaign would be ended by the autumn of 1941, before the first frost, and we are simply not equipped at all for this kind of weather.' To make his point stronger, he insisted that I should examine his lamentable uniform, his tattered shoes, and his fingers, covered with painful-looking blisters. His hands looked as if they had been burned all over.

But with the return of spring the attack recommenced. Once again Leningrad was subjected to attack by aircraft, artillery and infantry. In the far south the Germans captured the Crimea with its historically important naval base at Sebastopol. Three Russian armies were defeated

52   Columns of German prisoners passing through the ruins of Stalingrad after the Russian victory there.

at Kharkov, the important city of Rostov was captured and in August 1942 the Germans closed in for the attack on Stalingrad, which was heavily bombarded from the air throughout the summer and autumn (picture 49).

The Germans had reached the banks of the River Volga when the winter came, once more, to Russia's aid. The Luftwaffe was unable to fly; tanks did not roll and the Russians, spurred on by Stalin's call for a patriotic war, flung everything into, first, the defence, and then a massive counter-attack in which the German besiegers were themselves encircled, cut off from supplies and slowly starved or froze to death. More than 240 000 Germans died before the German commander, Von Paulus, surrendered on 1 February 1943 in what was Russia's greatest victory to date (picture 52).

helped by the Russian air force, now enjoying a numerical superiority over the Luftwaffe. The invasion from the west had led to the loss of many of Russia's industrial centres. Some industries had been moved to safer regions behind the Urals (p. 76) and Russian workers had rallied to the call for greater efforts so that the Russian forces had a more than adequate supply of war materials in 1943 and 1944.

The Germans were also under attack from the west after the first Allied landings in Normandy on 6 June 1944. Their forces along the Russian front were weakened, their spirits lowered by defeat and retreat, and were under constant attack from the now confident Russians. Russian armies liberated Poland, Romania, Bulgaria, Czechoslovakia and Austria before they met up with the Allied forces attacking Germany from the west. On 7 May the German commander, Keitel, surrendered to Marshal Zhukov and the great war was over (picture 54).

THE COUNTER-ATTACK

The Russians had the benefit of massive aid from the USA and Britain. In particular, they had the advantage of new, high-clearance trucks which carried the infantry in the wake of the new Russian tanks which were protected and

THE COST OF THE WAR

There is evidence that some Russians had welcomed the German invasion but that the Germans had behaved so brutally that even anti-Stalinists were converted into pro-Russian patriots. At least three million Russian civilians

53 German prisoners emerging from a dug-out. The Russian steamroller was pushing towards the Fatherland.

were killed by the occupying Germans and thousands of Russian families were taken to Germany as slave-labour.

But the NKVD was angered by the way the people of the Ukraine and the Baltic provinces had welcomed the Germans. During the war, in an effort to limit such behavour, the NKVD deported eight national minority groups from western Russia to remote regions of eastern Russia. Volga Germans, Crimean Tartars and others were uprooted. We know that about half the Crimean Tartars died as a result of this policy and that in all about 500 000 people from the eight minority groups perished.

For the majority of Russians the economic and social effects of the long war were very great. Food shortages, inflation, transport dislocation — it was 1916 and 1917 all over again (pp. 29, 31). On top of these problems there were the effects of the large-scale bombing and sieges.

72

One traveller wrote:

... from Moscow to the new frontier at Brest-Litovsk, for hundreds of miles, for thousands, there was not a standing or living object to be seen. Every town was flat, every city ... no barns ... no machinery ... no stations, no water-towers, not a solitary telegraph pole left .... All along the line lay twisted rails pulled up by the Germans.... In the unkempt fields ... women, children, very old men could be seen working with hand tools.

The houses all being gone, the people were living in dug-outs ... roofed over with fir branches .... Millions lived like this, not only all over the countryside but also amid the ruins of the great cities .... The people ... were dressed in rags; no boots or shoes .... There was very little food; the starvation years of 1941-42 were over but nearly everyone was hungry.

It would require a great deal of effort to get Russia back on its feet again.

54   A meeting of Russian soldiers at the Brandenburg
Gate, Berlin, 2 May 1945. On the tank, the poet Yevgeni
Dolmatov reads verses to the soldiers, who have fought
their way into the German capital.

YOUNG HISTORIAN

A

1 Write a paragraph on each of the follow-
ing: Russian invasion of Poland, 1919;
Western suspicion of the Comintern;
Litvinov; the Ukraine.

2 How did the Treaty of Rapallo benefit (a)
Russia, (b) Germany?

3 Give an account of the Treaty of Locarno
from the point of view of (a) Britain, (b)
France and (c) Russia.

4 Was Russia justified in becoming increasingly suspicious of the western democracies in the 1920s and 1930s?

5 Explain the signing of the Nazi-Soviet
Pact, 1939. Why was the rest of the world
surprised by the news of this Pact?

6 Explain (a) the early successes made by
Germany in 1941 and 1942, (b) why the
advance into Russia was halted and (c) the
reasons for the Russian victory after 1943.

B

1 Write the letter which might have been sent by Litvinov in which he explains his policy of increasing trade with the West and of the link between this and the need for collectivization (Chapter 6).

2 Write the letters which might have been sent by (a) a Russian and (b) a German who was at the negotiations leading up to the Treaty of Rapallo.

3 Write the letter which might have been sent by a German who believed that Germany ought to attack Russia.

4 Write the letters which might have been sent by a Ukrainian (a) on hearing of the German invasion; (b) after the Germans had mis-treated the civilian population.

5 Write the letter which might have been sent by a Russian peasant as he prepared to evacuate his village in the face of a German attack.

6 Write the letters which might have been sent from (a) Leningrad and (b) Stalingrad during the German sieges of those cities.

7 Write the letter which might have been written by a German soldier on the problem of fighting during the Russian winter.

8 Write the letter which a Russian soldier might have sent (a) during the attack on the Germans around Stalingrad, (b) after the German surrender in February 1943, (c) from liberated Hungary and (d) after he had reached Berlin.

C

Write the headlines which might have appeared above newspaper reports on:
(a) the Treaty of Rapallo — in Russian, German, British and French newspapers;
(b) the Treaty of Locarno — in German and Russian newspapers;
(c) the Nazi-Soviet Pact — in Russian, British and German newspapers;
(d) the Russian invasion of Poland, 1939 — in Russian, German and British newspapers;
(e) the German invasion of Russia — in Russian, German and British newspapers;
(f) German successes in Russia — in Russian, German and British newspapers;
(g) the German defeat at Stalingrad — in Russian and German newspapers;
(h) the Russian entry into Berlin;
(i) Keitel's surrender to Zhukov — in German and Russian newspapers.

D

1 On a large map mark (a) Russian gains, 1939-40; (b) German attacks, 1941-43; (c) Russian advances, 1943-45; (d) Russian gains, 1945.

2 Draw or paint a poster with the title: 'The Defence of the Motherland, 1942'.

STALIN'S LAST YEARS, 1945-1953

THE EFFECTS OF THE WAR

No other country suffered as badly as Russia during World War 2. Twenty million of her people died; millions of others were disabled. A large part of the work of the Five-Year Plans had been wiped out by German attacks and by Russia's own 'scorched earth' policy. Iron production was down by about half, steel by just under one half, railways had been torn up, power stations destroyed, farms devastated and millions of animals slaughtered. Over half of Russia's stock of housing had been destroyed and millions were homeless (picture 55).

55 Russian peasants watch as their homes are burnt by advancing Germans, December 1942.

In August 1945 the President, Kalinin, warned the people:

> . . . we cannot for one minute forget the basic fact that our country remains the one socialist state in the world . . . victory doesn't mean that all dangers to our state system and social order have disappeared. Only the . . . immediate danger which threatened us from Hitler's Germany has disappeared.

This fear of further attacks on 'our socialist state' and the need to rebuild that state for the benefit of its people and as an advertisement for the Communist philosophy lay behind the aims of the Fourth Five-Year Plan which was introduced by Stalin in August 1945:

> Not to mention the fact that the ration card system will be abolished in the near future, special attention will be given to the extension of production of consumer goods, to raising the standard of living of the working people by means of the steady reduction of the prices of all commodities and to extensive construction of scientific research institutes of all kinds which will enable science to deploy its forces.
> As to plans for a longer period, our party intends to organize a new powerful upsurge of the national economy which would enable us, for instance, to raise the level of our industry threefold compared with the pre-war level . . . .

RUSSIAN SUCCESSES

Most people thought that it would take Russia ten years to recover from the war. In fact by 1948 overall production was higher than it had been in 1940 and most of the damage done by the war had been made good. The old industrial centres had been rebuilt in the west while the newer centres behind the Urals were further developed. By 1950 Russia was producing 30 per cent more iron and 50 per cent more steel than she had produced in 1940, while the supply of electric power had doubled.

Many Russians had returned from service in the forces occupying parts of Europe and they reported on the high standard of living enjoyed in capitalist countries. The NKVD arrested, imprisoned or shot anyone caught spreading stories of capitalist success and Russian backwardness. But the Fourth Five-Year Plan took note of the need for the development of light industries which could produce the clothes, furniture and other consumer goods which would enable the Russians to enjoy a higher standard of living (picture 56).

AGRICULTURE

The one major problem area for the Russian planners was agriculture. A decree of 1946 made it clear that collectivization had failed. Too many peasants were not working as hard as they might on the collective farms, preferring to spend their time and energy on their private plots; collectively-owned machinery was mistreated, and too little attention was paid to providing incentives for the workers or fertilizers for the soil. The planners' answer was to increase the size of the collectives, to take the private plots away, to send dedicated Communists to work on the collectives and to extend the system of collectives into new areas. There was an increase in production of tractors and other farm machinery but in spite of all efforts and exhortations agricultural production remained low. While the Communists could organize great improvements in heavy and light industry, they seemed unable to do the same for agriculture.

TRANSPORT

During the war over 13 000 bridges had been destroyed. This gives some indication of the way in which the Russian transport system was affected by the war. By 1948 the railroad system had been restored to its 1940 capacity; by 1950 Russia had almost 50 per cent more railway capacity than it had in 1940, with new regions of Siberia and Soviet Asia being opened

up. There were 12 times as many diesel engines in use as there had been in 1940 although steam trains still did most of the work on Russian railways.

PURGES

After 1945 there was no revival of the mass purges of the 1930s, although the ethnic minorities suffered at the hands of the NKVD (p. 72). Under Beria's leadership the NKVD dealt strictly with anyone who showed any tendency to independence — in writing, the arts or in speech. Between 1946 and 1948 Zhdanov, governor of Leningrad during the siege (p. 70), led the campaign for orthodoxy; after his death in 1948 many of his associates were purged on the grounds that they had intrigued with Tito of Yugoslavia (p. 81). The creation of the state of Israel in 1948 led to an increase in anti-semitism in Russia (p. 92). In January 1953 nine doctors, seven of them Jews, were accused of having murdered Zhdanov. Later on Khrushchev was to say of this Doctors' Plot:

Actually there was no case except the declaration of the woman doctor Timashuk, who was probably influenced or ordered by someone to write Stalin a letter in which she declared that the doctors were applying allegedly improper methods of medical treatment. Such a letter was sufficient for Stalin to reach an immediate conclusion that there were doctor-plotters in the Soviet Union. He issued orders to arrest a group of eminent Soviet medical specialists. He personally issued advice on the conduct of the investigation of the arrested persons. He said Academician Vinogradov should be put in chains, another one should be beaten. Present at this Congress as a delegate was the former Minister of State Security, Comrade Ignatyev. Stalin told him curtly, 'If you do not obtain confessions from the doctors we will shorten you by a head.'

Stalin's death prevented a revival of the Terror of the 1930s, for according to Khrushchev, Stalin was on the point of carrying out a wholesale purge which would have led to the deaths of old colleagues, Voroshilov (who had led the prosecution during the 1930s), Molotov (the Foreign Minister (p. 54), and an Armenian, Mikoyan.

56 **Revolutionary Highway, one of the new streets in rebuilt Leningrad.**

STALIN, ROOSEVELT AND CHURCHILL

In companion volumes (*Europe in the Twentieth Century* and *The USA in the Twentieth Century*) it is shown how Britain and the USA cooperated with each other almost from the start of the European war in September 1939. Roosevelt and Churchill had had several important meetings both before and after the entry of the USA into the war. In November 1943 Stalin joined them at their meeting at Teheran in Persia and at a later conference at Yalta in February 1945 (picture 57). These were Stalin's first discussions with eminent politicians from the West. His attitude to the two leaders and to the discussions was coloured by his longstanding suspicion of the West (pp. 66-7). He told a Yugoslav: 'Perhaps you think that because we are Allies of the English, we have forgotten who they are and who Churchill is', indicating that he himself had not forgotten the English support of the Whites after 1918 (pp. 47). At Teheran he refused to believe that the Western Allies were unable to mount an invasion of France in 1943. Their refusal to do so left Russia to face the military might of Germany. Even when the invasion did take place in June 1944 Stalin believed that the Allies had acted only out of fear — of Russian success and of the possibility of Russian occupation of the whole of Europe.

STALIN AND POLAND

At the Yalta Conference the three wartime leaders reached a number of important decisions:
1 Germany was to be divided between the Allied Powers, each occupying an agreed zone;
2 Stalin agreed to enter the war against Japan within three months of the defeat of Germany;
3 The peoples of countries formerly occupied by Germany were to be given the chance to choose the kind of government they wanted;
4 A conference was to be held in April 1945 at San Francisco to finalize the details for the creation of the United Nations' Organisation;
5 The boundaries of the new post-war Poland were to be different from those of pre-war Poland. Russia was to be given a large slice of what had been eastern Poland and in return the new Poland was to include extensive and valuable territory which had once been German, taking the new Poland up to the Oder and Neisse Rivers.

◄ **57** Churchill, Roosevelt and Stalin at the Yalta Conference, February 1945.

58 Soviet troops welcomed in the Bulgarian capital, Sofia, September 1944.
▼

RUSSIA AND THE LIBERATION OF EASTERN EUROPE

The Russian armies drove the Germans from their own native land and out of the Eastern European countries which Germany had once occupied (picture 58). Romania, Bulgaria and Hungary had entered the war on the German side. The Russians treated these as enemy countries which were to be 'occupied' by the Red Army. Poland, Austria and Czechoslovakia had never sided with the Germans. The Russians claimed that these were 'liberated' countries. How far would Stalin agree to carry out the spirit of the Yalta agreement?

In the case of the 'occupied' countries Russia imposed her own terms. Frontiers were altered to Russia's advantage; Russian-controlled governments were imposed on the people. The Russians argued that their country had been devastated by the invasions of two World Wars. In 1945 they were intent, it was claimed, on the creation of a buffer of friendly countries between Russia and her potential enemies further west.

The 'liberated' countries were slightly more fortunate. Austria, like Germany, was divided into four zones. The Russians stripped their zone of its industrial goods to help in the redevelopment of their own war-shattered economy (pp. 72, 75-6). They did agree with the other

occupying powers to the formation of a democratically elected government for the whole country. Czechoslovakia was given back most of her pre-war territory and the Russians allowed elections which led to the formation of a government for the whole country. Dr Beneš became President, and the Prime Minister of a coalition government was the Communist, Klement Gottwald. In Poland the Russians suppressed the People's Party which represented peasant interests, broke up other political parties and forced them to join the National Front of the Polish Workers Party which was in fact a communist-led Party. Even in Czechoslovakia Dr Beneš was

forced to agree to the banning of the Agrarian Party and to the appointment of Communists to important government posts which gave them control of the police, communications (including radio) and the armed forces.

All this was contrary to the spirit of the Yalta agreement. Western politicians were alarmed at the way in which Russia had imposed close control over vast areas of Eastern Europe. Some saw this as the first stage in the Russian conquest of the whole of Europe.

59 The Soviet Union and her allies since 1945.

USA VERSUS RUSSIA, 1947-49

Stalin had agreed that Greece should be regarded as a British sphere of influence. After 1946 there was a civil war in which the Greek Communists, aided by neighbouring Communist countries, tried to overthrow the government of right-wing monarchists who had won the majority of seats in the 1946 elections. By 1947 Britain had to admit that she no longer had the economic or military strength required to put an end to this Communist uprising. President Truman of the USA then announced, in March 1947, that the USA would 'support free peoples who are resisting attempted subjection by armed minorities or by outside pressures.'

This 'Truman Doctrine' was seen by the Russians as an unwarranted interference by the USA in the affairs of a continent far removed from the USA. When the US Secretary of State (George Marshall) announced that the USA would provide massive aid to help the war-shattered countries of Europe to rebuild and recover, Stalin refused to allow any of Russia's satellites to accept this aid. In 1949 Russia forced the countries in its sphere to join the Council for Mutual Economic Assistance (Comecon). This was a Russian attempt to provide an alternative to the US-inspired Marshall aid.

CZECHOSLOVAKIA, 1948

In spite of the presence of the Russian army the Czech Communists won only 38 per cent of the votes in the first post-war elections, which led to the formation of a coalition government (p. 80).

In February 1948 the three Western Allies made their zones of Germany into one unified region, hoping that this would enable economic recovery to take place. Stalin considered that this was a Western move to rebuild a powerful Germany — from whom Russia had suffered in two World Wars. His reaction was quick and brutal. In March the Foreign Minister, Jan Masaryk, son of the man who had founded the state in 1919, was found dead — having 'fallen out of a window'; the elections, due in March, were postponed while the Communists forced Beneš to change the government to give the Communists more power, particularly in local

government; student demonstrations against these changes were crushed by the Russian army; non-Communist political parties were banned and in the elections which took place in May 1948 the voters were presented with a single list of candidates, dominated by the Communist-led National Front. Having won the elections, the Communists then forced Beneš to resign and Gottwald was installed as President. This success was followed by a Stalinist-purge of the Czech Communist Party in which dozens of prominent leaders were arrested, imprisoned and executed. The main resistance to the Communist take-over came from the Catholic Church but in 1950 most monasteries were forcibly closed, Church property confiscated and Church leaders arrested. In 1951 Archbishop Berans, the most important Church leader, was expelled from the country which then had to settle down to rule by Stalinists.

TITO OF YUGOSLAVIA

Yugoslavia had freed herself from German occupation largely by her own efforts and had not been occupied by Russian forces. Tito, leader of the Yugoslav Communist Party and leader of the anti-German forces during the war, was unwilling to take orders from Moscow. In 1948 the disagreement between Tito and Stalin came to a head when Tito refused to join a system of Balkan alliances under Russian domination or run his economy to suit Russian interests. In June 1948 Tito, his government and the Yugoslav Communist Party were expelled from the Russian-dominated Cominform, Stalin boasting to Khrushchev: 'I will shake my little finger and there will be no more Tito; he will fall.' He was wrong about this as Trotsky had been about world revolution (p. 64).

BERLIN, 1948-49

In 1947 the Russian Foreign Minister, Molotov, proposed that the four occupying powers should allow Germany to be reunified with a constitution based on the Weimar constitution of 1919.

As part of the price for this reunification Molotov asked that the Communist Party be allowed a number of posts in the new government and that the Western Powers pay Russia the ten billion dollars which she claimed was due to her from Germany. The Americans, British and French refused these demands and in 1948 united their own three zones to form Western Germany where two political parties were established. The Russians then established a Communist-dominated government for Eastern Germany. Berlin lies in Eastern Germany and in February 1948 the Soviet Commander there claimed that the whole of Berlin should now be regarded as part of the Russian-dominated Eastern Germany. This was Russia's answer to the Western decision to form the Federal Republic of Western Germany and to their decision to revalue the German mark as part of the attempt to stamp out the black market and to help the economic recovery of Western Germany. The Russians forbade the distribution or circulation of this currency in their zone and in June announced that the railways and roads into Berlin from the west would be closed. The blockade lasted for a year and the supplying of the city was a costly business as the Western Powers had to take everything in by air (picture 60).

60 Stores being loaded by German workers, under British army command, in Hanover during the Berlin airlift, 1948.

During the year it seemed that war must break out between East and West as the Russians tried to prevent aircraft flying to Berlin and the Americans in particular showed that they were not going to be bullied into withdrawal. In May 1949 the Russians announced that the roads into Berlin from the west were once again to be opened. In August 1949 the western Federal German Republic was set up and in October the eastern German Democratic Republic was established under the leadership, first of the Socialist Grotewohl, then — after his resignation — of the hard-line Stalinist Communist, Ulbricht.

NATO

In March 1948 Britain, France and the Benelux countries signed the Treaty of Brussels, a defensive alliance based partly on the fear of a revived Germany and partly on fear of Russian domination of Europe. But the countries of the Brussels Pact had only a dozen divisions to put into the field against over 250 divisions of the Communist countries. Bevin, British Foreign Secretary, had already learned, in Greece, that Britain could not go it alone against Communism. Nor did he and the other leaders of Western Europe believe that they could stand up to Russia. The Berlin airlift had succeeded only because of American money, planes and determination.

In the first years after the war the Americans had seemed to be on the point of retreating once again into isolation, leaving Europe to its own devices. It was Russian aggression — in Poland, Hungary, Greece and Berlin — which brought them back into European affairs. In April 1949 the North Atlantic Treaty Organisation was formed. It included the members of the Brussels Treaty and the USA, Canada, Denmark, Norway, Iceland, Italy and Portugal. In 1953 Greece and Turkey became members of this Organisation, which had its headquarters at Fontainebleau, near Paris.

The Western Powers claimed that NATO was only a defensive organization. The Russians saw it as an American attempt to dominate Europe and to prepare for an attack on Russia. The power of NATO was limited in the sense that it never had ground forces equal to those of the Communist countries; it did have, however, the might of America which possessed the atomic bomb. In 1949 the Russians exploded their first atomic bomb and so brought to an end the American monopoly of this terrible weapon and lessened the power of NATO.

The next stage in the East-West conflict occurred in the Far East. Korea had been divided into two parts at the end of World War 2 — the Russians having control of the northern part and the Americans controlling the southern half. In 1949 both countries withdrew their forces and fighting broke out between north and south. The Korean War led to the despatch of a United Nations Force under American leadership and how this almost led to a war between America and China. Here we should notice that as far as the Western Powers were concerned, Korea was an attempt by the Russians to extend their influence, to break the Americans and other Western Powers. The war was brought to an end by a cease-fire on 27 July 1953, a date which marks the beginning of the end of that Cold War which had marked relationships between East and West since 1945.

STALIN'S DEATH AND A RE-ASSESSMENT

Stalin died in March 1953, having ruled Russia for almost 30 years. His body was put in a place of honour alongside Lenin's in the mausoleum in Red Square, Moscow. In the next chapter we will see how Russia changed after his death. Here we ought to note that in 1956 his successor surprised the world with a violent attack on Stalin's policies and methods. In his speech at the 20th Party Congress, Khrushchev condemned his personal dictatorship, the great purges of the 1930s and his quarrel with Tito. In this surprising speech, Khrushchev said:

Stalin became even more capricious, irritable, and brutal; in particular his suspicion grew. His persecution mania reached unbelievable dimensions. Many workers were becoming enemies before his very eyes. After the war, Stalin separated himself from the collective even more. Everything was decided by him alone without any consideration for anyone or anything.

However, even Khrushchev was forced to say:

In the past, Stalin undoubtedly performed

61   Cartoon showing a 'saintly' Khrushchev crowning Stalin's statue with the corpses of victims of purges and persecutions.

great services to the Party, to the working class and to the international workers' movement .... Stalin was convinced that this [the Terror], was necessary for the defence of the interests of the working class against the plotting of the enemies and against the attack of the imperialist camp .... We cannot say that these were the deeds of a giddy despot. He considered that this should be done in the interests of the Party, of the working masses, in the name of defence of the revolution's gains. In this lies the whole tragedy!

YOUNG HISTORIAN

A

1 Give an account of Russian treatment of the countries of Eastern Europe to bring out (a) why some people thought it was contrary to the Yalta agreement and (b) Stalin's reasons for this treatment.

2 Give a brief account of the relationship between Russia and (a) Poland and (b) Czechoslovakia between 1945 and 1953.

3 Trace the development of the Cold War using as your guidelines Yalta, the Truman Doctrine, Czechoslovakia, Berlin, Korea.

4 Examine the crisis over Berlin to show (a) why the Russians created the crisis; (b) why the Western Powers responded as they did; (c) how the crisis was resolved.

5 Make a list of the capitals of the countries lying behind the Iron Curtain (picture 65). Explain why it was easier for Stalin to impose his will on Poland than on Yugoslavia.

6 Write a paragraph on each of the following: The Fourth Five-Year Plan; the Doctors' Plot; the 20th Party Congress; Tito.

B

1 Write the letter which might have been sent by a Russian praising the recovery of his country after 1945.

2 Write the letter which might have been sent by someone who was afraid of a renewal of the purges in 1953.

3 Write the letters which might have been sent by (a) a Russian and (b) a Pole concerning Russia's treatment of his country since 1945.

4 Write the letter which might have been sent by a Russian who wanted to justify the way in which his country stripped many countries of their industrial goods after 1945.

5 Write the letters which might have been written by (a) a Czech democrat and (b) a Czech Communist after the death of Jan Masaryk.

6 Write the letters which might have been sent during the Berlin Airlift by (a) a West Berliner; (b) an RAF pilot flying goods into Berlin; (c) a Russian on duty in Berlin.

7 Write the letter which might have been sent by a delegate at the 20th Party Congress.

C

Write the headlines which might have appeared above newspaper reports on:

(a) Stalin's death — in Russian, Yugoslavian and American newspapers;

(b) the end of the Yalta Conference — in Russian, British and US newspapers and in newspapers published by Polish exiles;

(c) the liberation of Prague, 1945 — in Russian and Czech newspapers;

(d) the formation of the National Front government in Czechoslovakia — in Russian, British and Czech-democrat newspapers;

(e) Tito's expulsion from the Cominform — in Russian and Yugoslavian newspapers;

(f) the closure of land approaches to Berlin — in Russian, West German and US newspapers;

(g) the Berlin airlift — in Russian and West Berlin newspapers;

(h) the end of the Berlin crisis — in Russian and US newspapers;

(i) the start of the Korean War — in Chinese, Russian and US newspapers.

MODERN SOVIET RUSSIA, 1953-1976

STALIN'S SUCCESSORS

Russia's new leaders, Malenkov and Khrushchev, quickly showed that Russia was to be run differently. Beria, Stalin's Chief of Secret Police, was executed and the powers of the secret police reduced. Malenkov tried to increase the production of consumer goods to provide a higher standard of living. This was opposed by many of his colleagues in the government and at the beginning of 1955 he resigned, to be replaced, as Prime Minister, by Bulganin.

AGRICULTURE

In an attempt to provide more food, Khrushchev announced in 1954 that the area under cultivation was to be increased — mainly by the addition of five million acres of 'virgin lands' in Siberia and Kazakhstan. 350 000 Young Communists were 'volunteered' to help, and two good harvests increased the total Russian grain production by 70 per cent between 1955 and 1958. However the scheme disappointed as soil erosion swept away the fertile top-soil, and Russia's grain output slumped again. This was one reason for Khrushchev's fall from power in 1964, by which time many Russian towns had been forced to introduce bread-rationing and Russia had to import huge quantities of grain.

62 Combine harvesters at work on a gigantic state farm in Kazakhstan.

INDUSTRY

At the 22nd Party Congress of 1961 Khrushchev boasted:

I would remind you that a mere ten or eleven years ago Soviet industrial output was less than that of the USA. At the present time the USSR has already outstripped the United States in the extraction of iron ore and coal, the production of coke, prefabricated concrete elements, heavy diesel and electric locomotives, sawn timber, woollen textiles, sugar, butter, fish, and a number of other items.

Our country now accounts for almost a

fifth of the world's industrial output, or more than Britain, France, Italy, Canada, Japan, Belgium and the Netherlands combined. Yet these are all highly developed countries with a total population of 280 000 000. The fact that our country with a population of 220 000 000 has surpassed them in total volume of industrial production shows how swiftly and surely Socialist economy is progressing.

The implementation of the Seven-Year Plan will bring our country up to such a level that little more time will be required to outstrip the United States economically. By fulfilling this basic economic task the Soviet Union will achieve an historic victory in the peaceful competition with the United States of America.

However, as his critics point out, he did not explain that many of the goods he mentioned are no longer regarded as very important in the USA. Nor did Khrushchev say that Russian industry was failing to reach its planned targets in electricity and gas, plastics, turbines, diesel engines, all of which are more important in industrial terms than woollen textiles.

THE COLONIAL REVOLUTIONS, 1953

In 1948 Stalin had purged the Polish Communist Party of about 70 000 members, along with Party Secretary, Gomulka, suspected of being a Titoist (p. 81). In 1951 Gomulka was imprisoned by the Polish government, which also attacked the powerful Catholic Church by insisting that all clerical appointments had to be approved by the government.

Stalin's death led to changes in Poland. The government was forced to allow more freedom to press and radio and to curtail the activities of the secret police. Gomulka was released, and appointed First Secretary of the Party in 1956.

While Stalin was alive, the government of Hungary became increasingly Communist. Non-Communist members were hounded from office, the Prime Minister, Nagy, resigning in 1947. Here, as in Poland, the government attacked the Catholic Church, whose leader, Cardinal Mindszenty, was arrested, tortured (p. 62) and imprisoned. After Stalin's death, Nagy was brought back as Prime Minister and, as in Czechoslovakia, there was a slowing down of collectivization of land. In Poland there was decollectivization in 1956.

88

In Czechoslovakia the workers at the Skoda works in Pilsen greeted the news of the death of their Stalinist leader, Gottwald, by strikes and demonstrations for better wages. The rioters were attacked by police and the army, and the riots quickly brought under control. However, the government took notice of the discontent. More consumer goods were produced and collectivization slowed down.

On 14 May 1953 the government of East Germany announced that workers would have to produce ten per cent more and for the same wages. The building workers of East Berlin downed tools and called for a protest march on 16 June (picture 64). This led to even greater demonstrations on the following day when crowds tore down the Red Flag at the Brandenburg Gate. Russian tanks had to be brought in to disperse the worker-demonstrators and peace was restored. But the peace was an uneasy one — in East Germany, Poland, Hungary and Czechoslovakia.

CO-EXISTENCE WITH CAPITALISM

Relaxation in Russia and the satellite countries was accompanied by the development of new attitudes towards the countries of the West. This change in policy was due in part to a change in leadership in Russia. It was also due to a new confidence in Russia itself which now realized that it was in a position to challenge the technological power of the USA, having outstripped in economic terms the countries of Western Europe whose money had once been essential to get Russian industry on its feet (p. 8). An outward sign of Russian progress was the launching of the first satellite into space in October 1957. As Senator Lyndon Johnson of the USA said, 'We've got to admit that the Soviets have beaten us at our own game.'

Bulganin and Khrushchev undertook many visits overseas, to Western European countries and the USA, no longer — it seemed — the enemy it had been during the Stalinist period of the Cold War

In 1953 Russia agreed to an armistice in Korea. A meeting of foreign ministers of the USA, Britain, France and Russia in Geneva in

64   Red Army tanks open fire in East Berlin, 18 June 1953, when Berlin workers rose in rebellion against the Soviet government.

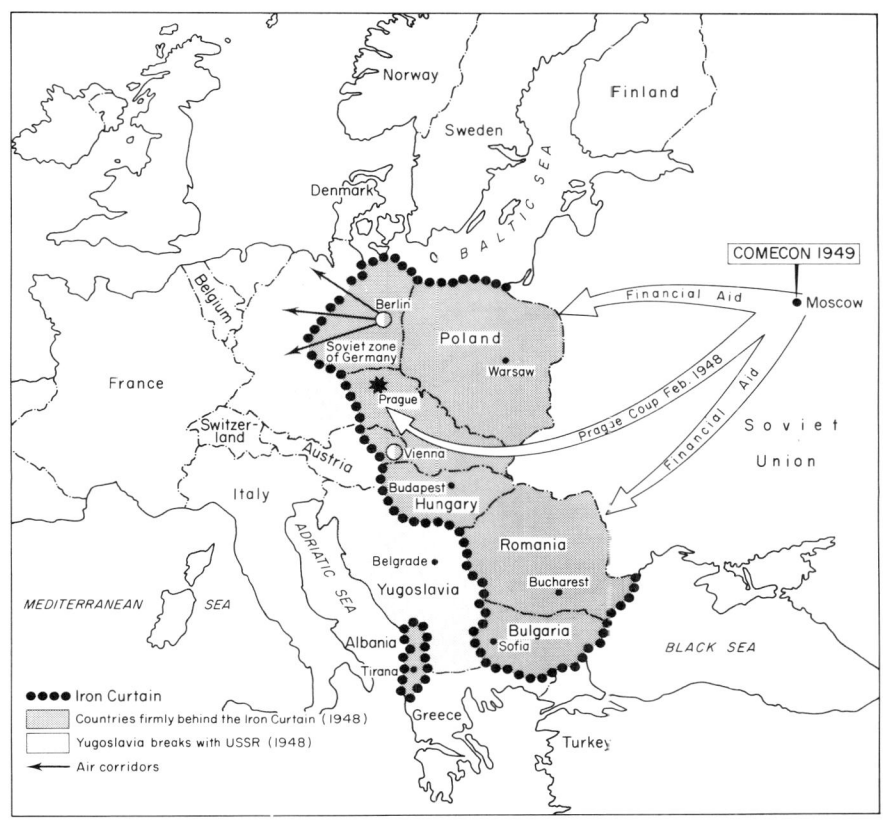

65   The Iron Curtain.

July 1955 discussed the possibilities of disarmament in a friendly atmosphere: 'the spirit of Geneva' was used to describe the change that had taken place in international relations since 1953. However, Western Germany was admitted by NATO (p. 83), and Russia drew up the Warsaw Pact which committed the countries of Eastern Europe to a 20-year period of 'Friendship, Cooperation and Mutual Assistance', and which permitted Russia to keep troops in certain of the countries in the Pact.

In 1959 Khrushchev visited President Eisenhower at his holiday home at Camp David and agreed to calling a Summit Meeting in Paris in 1960. Eisenhower, Khrushchev, Macmillan (Britain) and de Gaulle (France) attended the Paris Summit in the hope that they could solve the Berlin problem (p. 81), begin negotiations on nuclear disarmament and on relations between NATO and the Warsaw Pact countries. However, this Summit never got started because of Russian anger over the U2 'spy-plane' incident. A US plane piloted by Gary Powers was shot down over Russian territory. Powers was put on trial, and confessed to being engaged in taking photographs of Russian military installations. The Russians demanded that Eisenhower apologise for this 'attack' on Russia, condemn those who had ordered it and promise that it would not be repeated. Eisenhower refused to be bullied publicly, Khrushchev refused to allow the Summit to get under way and so nothing came of the most important international meeting since 1945.

Khrushchev met the new US President, John Kennedy, in Vienna in June 1961 but once again there was no solution to the Berlin problem and it seemed as if Khrushchev took away the impression that he would be able to force the young and inexperienced President to do as he wished. This helps to explain the Cuba crisis (p. 92).

66 Russian tanks in Budapest, 1956.

1956-YEAR OF CRISIS

At the 20th Party Congress in 1956 Khrushchev denounced Stalin (p. 83). One reason for this attack was the emergence in the government of a number of critics who, in 1957, managed to out-vote Khrushchev who then appealed to the Central Committee of the Party for support. Marshal Zhukov (p. 70) supported Khrushchev, his critics, Malenkov, Molotov (p. 77), Bulganin and others were removed from office so that Khrushchev became the sole leader of Russia.

The condemnation of Stalin led to similar de-nunciation of Stalinist practices in Czechoslovakia and Poland where 30 000 political prisoners were freed. Polish workers used this relaxation as an excuse for industrial action. An uprising in Poznan in June 1956 was put down by police and troops. The reinstatement of the more liberal Gomulka (p. 88) led to the development of a more liberal regime in which the Church was allowed to operate more freely, Parliament was given more power, workers consulted more often about industrial plans, and writers and artists

allowed greater freedom. The Communist Party remained firmly in charge, however, and over the years many of the reforms were undone by Gomulka and his followers.

The Russians were worried about developments in Poland. Worse was to follow in Hungary, where a bad harvest and food shortages added to the unrest caused by the denunciation of Stalin. Demonstrations on 23 October against the government, the secret police and the agrarian policy led to Nagy becoming Prime Minister again (p. 88) and the promise of free elections, withdrawal from the Warsaw Pact (p. 89) and the release of Cardinal Mindszenty (p. 88). On 30 October the Russians seemed to have accepted what had happened; the Russian army moved out of Budapest. But on 4 November they made a massive attack on the capital in which 25 000 people were killed, the government overthrown, Nagy arrested — to be executed later on. Russia was not going to allow free elections or the weakening of the Warsaw Pact.

67 A policeman in the Western sector of Berlin talking to a Communist policeman on the other side of the rough wall built in August 1961 to prevent refugees making their way from East to West. This rough wall has been replaced by a more finished and better guarded one.

90

RUSSIA AND CHINA

Russia had welcomed the success of Mao Tse-tung and the Chinese Communists (explained in a companion volume on *China in the Twentieth Century*). Russian technicians and scientists helped develop Chinese industry after 1949. However, after 1956, the Chinese began to accuse the Russians of 'revisionism' of being 'soft-liners' as compared to Lenin and Stalin and of being 'running-mates' of the West with which Russia was trying to work out the policy of co-existence. In 1960 Russia withdrew all the experts at work in China and stopped supplying China with badly needed goods. In 1964 China exploded its own atomic bomb, so becoming a member of the 'big league'. In both countries there were propaganda campaigns aimed at the other; border disputes became more frequent and sometimes led to local fighting. One beneficiary of this Russo-Chinese quarrel was the USA which tried to be friendly with both and which helped bring China into UNO.

BERLIN

Berlin remained as a bone of contention between Russia and the West. In 1959 Khrushchev recognized East Germany's claim to control of the whole of the city, demanded the withdrawal of the Western Powers from West Berlin and threatened that if they did not do so he would sign a separate peace treaty with East Germany. The threat failed; the Western Powers did not withdraw nor did Khrushchev sign a separate peace treaty. In 1959, 1960 and 1961 steps were taken to try to solve the Berlin problem (p. 89). In August 1961 the East Germans began the building of the massive Berlin Wall, largely to check the flow of East Germans to the West. The Wall remains a sign of the division of Germany and of East-West hostility (picture 67).

CUBA, 1962

From 1956 until 1959 Fidel Castro had led an uprising against the pro-American but dictatorial government led by Batista. In 1959 Batista fled and Castro set up a Socialist government. The USA tried to overthrow this Socialist-on-the-doorstep by banning all trade between the USA and Cuba and, when this had little effect, by supporting an invasion by Cuban refugees in 1961. The failure of this 'Bay of Pigs' adventure confirmed US anger with Cuba and showed the Cubans that their only friend was Russia, which then established missile bases on the island. Russia and Cuba argued that these were for defensive purposes; Kennedy and the American people believed that they were intended to frighten the USA.

In the autumn of 1962 the US government had evidence of the existence of the bases from photographs taken by a U2 spy-plane. Kennedy then demanded that Russia dismantle the bases and remove the missiles. He put a naval blockade around the island and threatened to attack any Russian ship trying to get to Cuba. There was a very real danger that this might have led to war between Russia and the USA. At the last moment Khrushchev ordered Russian ships to turn back and agreed to the removal of the rockets.

KHRUSHCHEV'S DOWNFALL

In 1964 Khrushchev fell from power against an opposition which had grown increasingly stronger and more outspoken at the failure of his policies — in agriculture (p. 87) as well as in the field of consumer goods. The more fervent Communists resented his soft line towards the West which had led to quarrels with China. In October 1964 he was voted out of power and a triumvirate of Kosygin, Brezhnev and Podgorny voted in.

While there was little change of policy in industry and agriculture, there was a distinct sign of changes as regards dissidents and the Jews. Since 1956 there had emerged a number of outspoken critics of Communism in general and of its application in Russia in particular. Khrushchev himself had supported the proposal to publish Solzhenitsyn's *One Day in the Life of Ivan Denisovich* in 1962. Russia's new leaders were less liberal and a number of critics have been arrested, tried and imprisoned while many have been sent to mental hospitals, as if to criticize were a sign of mental imbalance.

1968, ANOTHER YEAR OF CRISIS

The unrest in Russia's colonies or satellites came to a head again in 1968. A liberal-Communist Dubček became First Secretary of the Czech Communist Party in 1967, carried in to power on the wave of discontent that swept Czechoslovakia arising from low wages, high prices, long hours, food shortages and too tight state control over large sections of life. The hard-line President Novotny was forced to resign in January 1968 and his successor — the popular General Svoboda — worked with Dubček to introduce sweeping reforms. Workers were free to form unions, political parties were legalized and allowed to hold meetings, the press censorship was ended, the activities of the secret police restricted, political prisoners freed and plans made for a democratically elected Parliament.

During the summer of 1968 troops from the Warsaw Pact countries held their manoeuvres inside and around Czechoslovakia. In August Russian and other Warsaw Pact troops invaded the country, resistance was quickly crushed and Dubček flown as a prisoner to Moscow. However, the Russians could find no one to form a government whilst he was in prison. On his release he was again a member of the government but had to accept the repeal of most of his earlier reforms and the occupation of his country by Russian troops. In 1969 Dubček was dismissed, later to be deprived of his Party membership. His successor, Dr Husak, promised the Russians that he would follow a harder line. For the moment the Russians and their satellite leaders appear to be in control but the increasing evidence of dissidence inside Russia and of anti-Russian sentiments inside the satellites makes it likely that there will be future crises like those of 1953, 1956 and 1968.

THE 1970s

Nor have things got much better inside Russia itself. There has been a sustained and organized campaign by writers and other intellectuals critical of the illiberalism of the Soviet government. In Stalin's time such dissidents were executed, imprisoned or interned in lunatic asylums. The present Soviet government has not executed its critics. It has, however, followed the Stalinist practice of imprisonment as well as condemning people to long stays in lunatic asylums. However, the government has also shown itself to be conscious of world opinion in a way that Stalin never was. Some dissidents have been allowed to leave Russia; some of the trials of other dissidents have been held in public and Western observers allowed to attend and to write about the trials. The present regime seems to be caught in a trap of its own making. On the one hand it is unwilling to take the Stalinist line of ruthlessly stamping out the opposition; on the other hand it is incapable of allowing the opposition a free voice.

One reason for the continual criticism of the regime is that it quite clearly has failed to 'deliver the goods'. Never was this more obvious than in 1972 and 1975 when the collectivized agricultural system failed to produce enough grain to feed the Russian people. The Russian government was forced to buy vast quantities of wheat and other grains from the USA and Canada, the homes of free enterprise. Ironically, this had the effect of driving up wheat prices throughout the non-communist world and was a factor in stoking up the inflationary spiral which has so badly affected Britain and other Western countries since 1972.

But until the early 1970s it seemed that it was not only agriculture that had disappointed. The regime seemed to have lost whatever drive Russian Communism may have had. Whereas Trotsky and other early leaders talked about 'world revolution' and Khrushchev boasted that Russia 'will bury you', the present regime seemed merely content to hold on to power inside Russia. The outside world had apparently rejected its brand of Communism which had clearly failed to solve Russian economic and social problems as the increasing volume of dissidence revealed.

Until the early 1970s this was true, but Soviet foreign policy in Africa, especially in Angola and Ethiopia has been very adventurous since the mid-1970s.

After the fall of Khrushchev in 1964 Russia was led by a triumvirate of Kosygin, the Prime

68 A summary of the unrest in Russia's satellites. In Berlin, Budapest and Prague the might of the Red Army was needed to crush the dissidents.

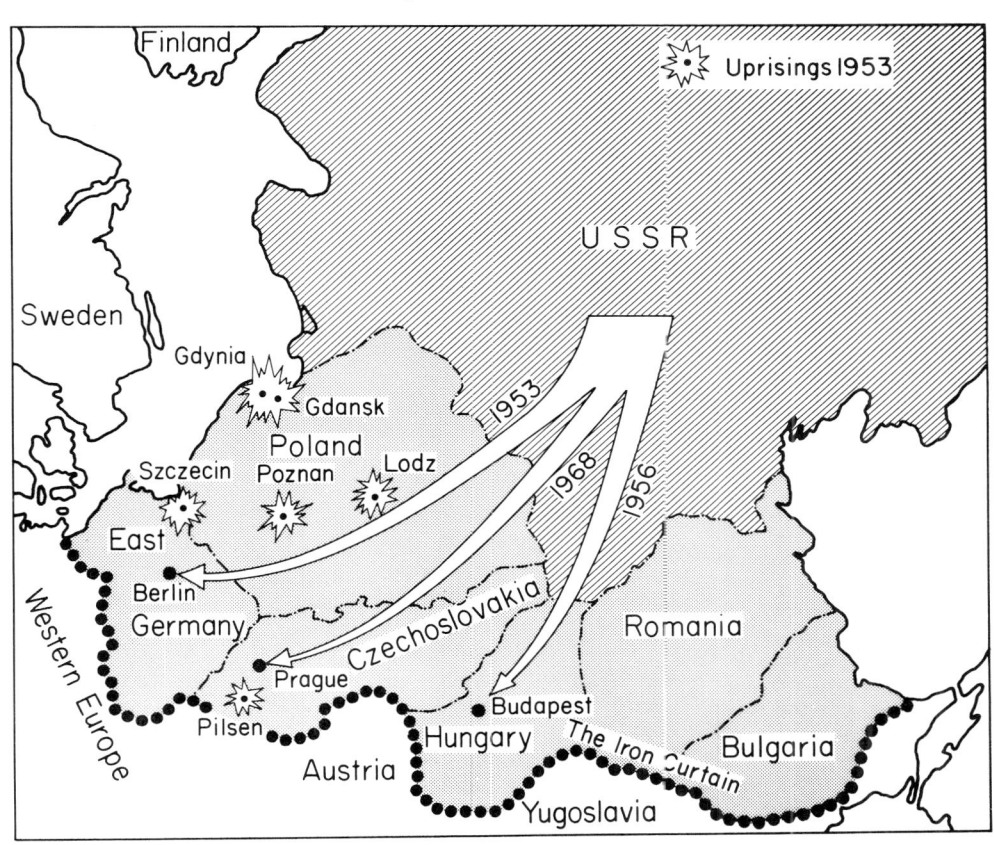

Minister, Brezhnev, the First Secretary of the Communist Party and Podgorny, the President. Never again, it seemed, would one man be allowed to dominate affairs. In 1961 the Soviet Union began discussion of a new constitution. It was published finally in 1977. We do not yet know how this will affect the ordinary Russians nor how far it will incorporate any of the changes demanded by dissidents. One thing we do know: in 1977 Brezhnev, the head of the Communist Party, had President Podgorny removed from office and 'accepted the invitation' to assume the office of President himself. Whatever changes the new constitution may make there seems little doubt that the Communist Party of the Soviet Union, representing a minority of Russians, will continue to dominate the political system, and, through it, the economic and social systems also.

YOUNG HISTORIAN

A

1 What were the reasons behind the development of the 'virgin land'? Why was this project a disappointment? What is the significance of Russia's need to import grain from Canada and the USA?

2 Examine Khrushchev's statement on Russian industry (p. 87) and then show:
   (a) that this was the result of Stalin's Five-Year Plan;
   (b) that it helped provide the Russians with a rising standard of living;
   (c) that Russia still lagged behind the USA.

3 Discuss Russia's relations with (a) Poland and (b) Hungary from 1953 to 1968. What is the significance of the unrest in these countries?

4 Discuss the nature of the unrest in Russia's European satellites in (a) 1953 and (b) 1968 and show how this unrest led to some reforms. How and why was the unrest suppressed?

5 Trace the development of relations between Russia and the USA after 1953.

6 Why did Berlin play a large part in international relations in this period? What attempts have been made to solve the Berlin problem? Why have they failed?

7 Write a paragraph on each of the following: Cuba; Dubček; Gomulka; Nagy.

B

1 Write the letter which might have been written by a Russian commenting on the fall of Malenkov.

2 Write the letters which might have been sent by (a) a Russian official and (b) a US official during the negotiations over the import of grain into Russia.

3 Write the letter which might have been sent by one of the Berlin rioters, 1953.

4 Write the letters which might have been sent from Paris in 1960 by (a) a Russian official and (b) a member of the US delegation.

5 Write the letters which a young Hungarian might have written in 1956 (a) before, (b) during and (c) after the uprising.

6 Write the letters which might have been written by (a) a Cuban and (b) an American about the installation of Russian missile bases in Cuba.

7 Write the letters which might have been sent by a young Czech (a) before, (b) during and (c) after the Russian and Warsaw Pact attack in 1968.

C

Write the headlines which might have appeared above newspaper reports on:
(a) the virgin lands scheme;
(b) import of grain into Russia;
(c) the re-instatement of Gomulka;
(d) the Pilsen riots;
(e) the launching of the first space satellite;
(f) the signing of the Warsaw Pact.
(g) the meeting between Khrushchev and Eisenhower, 1959;
(h) the Hungarian uprising, 1956;
(i) Russian suppression of the Hungarian uprising, 1956;
(j) the recall of Russian technicians from China;
(k) the building of the Berlin Wall;
(l) the trial of some of the Russian dissidents;
(m) the Russian and Warsaw Pact invasion of Prague, 1968.

INDEX

The numbers in **bold type** are the figure numbers of the illustrations